HIRE LIBRARIES

RUTH SLEIGH-JOHNSON

First published in Great Britain 2012
A&C Black Publishers
an imprint of Bloomsbury Publishing Plc
50 Bedford Square
London
WC1B 3DP

ISBN: 9781408133972

Copyright © Ruth Sleigh-Johnson 2012

A CIP catalogue record for this book is available from the British Library

Ruth Sleigh-Johnson has asserted her rights under the Copyright, Design and Patents Act, 1988, to be identified as the author of this work.

All rights reserved. No part of this publication may be reproduced in any form or by any means – graphic, electronic or mechanical, including photocopying, recording, taping or information storage and retrieval systems – without the prior permission in writing from the publishers.

This book is produced using paper that is made from wood grown in managed, sustainable forests. It is natural, renewable and recyclable. The logging and manufacturing processes conform to the environmental regulations of the country of origin.

Publisher: Susan James
Project manager: Davida Saunders
Assistant editor: Agnes Upshall
Cover design: Saffron Stocker
Page design: Evelin Kasikov
Proofreader: Jane Anson

Photography for Part 1 by Ruth Sleigh-Johnson unless otherwise stated.
Illustrations by Emelie Svensson

Please note that the dolls and creatures in this book contain small parts and are not suitable to be given to young children.

The patterns in this book are for your personal use and enjoyment only. Please respect the intellectual property of our contributors. Information given in this book is to the author's best knowledge and every effort has been made to ensure accuracy and safety but neither the author nor publisher can be held responsible for any resulting injury, damage or loss to either persons or property. Read through all the information in each chapter before commencing work. Any further information that will assist in updating of any future editions would be gratefully received.

Printed and bound in China

Contents

Acknowledgements

My sister and I always loved what we affectionately called 'the creatures', and they came on holidays to Swanage with us, had their own school, and even their own sports day!

It has been a real joy to create these new dolls and creatures, and I would like to thank all those who had the imagination and interest to spend time designing and making them too.

This book is dedicated to the memory of Bink, who encouraged us to be creative, and whose creativity is sadly missed. It is also for Bea and Rueben, who like making things.

Introduction

Handmade is the way to go! The recent trend for knitting while you natter, for 'upcycling' vintage furniture, and for reusing fabric buttons and trims from old clothes and accessories to create something new is not going away.

Stylish homes with an eclectic mix of old and modern feature the odd interesting piece that is totally different simply because it has been made by hand. These are often the most treasured gifts. There is such satisfaction in making something to cherish, either to give away or to keep, that it comes highly recommended by all who do it! Often becoming a maker of lovely things – and what better than an adorable doll or creature – is the start of a lifetime habit, one that is enjoyable and rewarding.

This book has hand-stitched projects for beginners with little sewing experience, as well as some more complicated dolls. For knitters there are some real treats in store. The creatures are small – allowing you the opportunity to use fabric and wool left over from larger projects – so you may not need to buy very much to make a start. Any of this selection of lovelies is sure to appeal to children, but they will also look good gracing a chair or in pride of place on a shelf.

Before you start, take inspiration from makers who earn a living from creating dolls and creatures, and also from the work of those who do it just for fun. The exciting part for me in making of these projects is giving them an outfit from fabric from a favourite old dress, and a face that brings the creature alive! Enjoy making dolls and creatures!

Part 1
Projects

1. Flat dolls

Handheld doll

This is the simplest of flat dolls – two fabric pieces sewn together and stuffed to form a hand-sized softie. It can be made from offcuts from any sewing project, but trims and fabric bought to remember special days out, events or celebrations can also be used, to give these little treasures a hidden meaning.

YOU WILL NEED

- 2 egg-shaped doll pieces (see p.133)
- 1 face piece
- 1 hair piece
- 2 ear pieces (a non-fraying fabric such as felt)
- Wings, if you are making the angel (a non-fraying fabric such as felt)
- Gold braid for the halo
- Trims, ribbons, buttons and beads

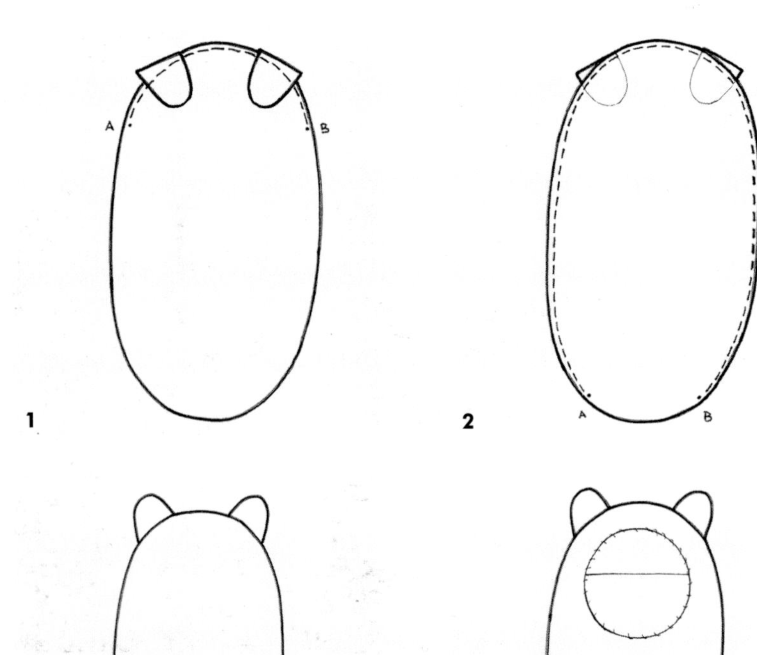

3

4

5

6

Place pattern pieces on fabric and cut out with care.

1 Place body pieces right sides together, with ears hanging down, as shown, sandwiched in between the two layers. Tack from A to B.

2 With a small running stitch or backstitch (more durable) sew from A to B leaving a 3cm (1¼in) opening at the base of the doll shape.

3 Turn to the right side. The ears will now 'pop up' into position. Stuff the doll.

4 Close the opening at the base of the doll by oversewing the gap. Place the face shape with the hair shape on top of it, and stitch through with a tiny stitch, securing all the layers to the body, while not pushing the needle into the stuffing. Instead make the stitches shallow.

5 Add trims of lace, ribbon or braid, using a tiny running stitch. Add stitched or appliquéd features to the face.

6 If you are making an angel, attach the wing piece at the back of the doll with a neat line of stitches, while some tiny stitches will also keep the braid, which forms a halo, in place. Adapt the pattern pieces a bit and you can make all sorts of creatures (see the owl on page 130, for inspiration).

Flat cat

This cat is made from velvet, but you can use any fabric. I also refer to him as a 'he' despite the fact that he is wearing a dress, probably because his face is quite masculine!

I used scraps of velvet to hand-stitch the shapes to the face; another option is hand embroidery, which works just as well – the choice is yours. The flat cat pattern is based on the two cats shown here, which have sat on my sister Jane's sofa for years and years.

Cats designed and made by Jane Seabrook.

YOU WILL NEED

- **2 cat pieces (see p.132)**
- **Dress and lining pieces**
- **Embroidery threads or shapes for appliqué.**

A class full of cats by Year 10 students.

1

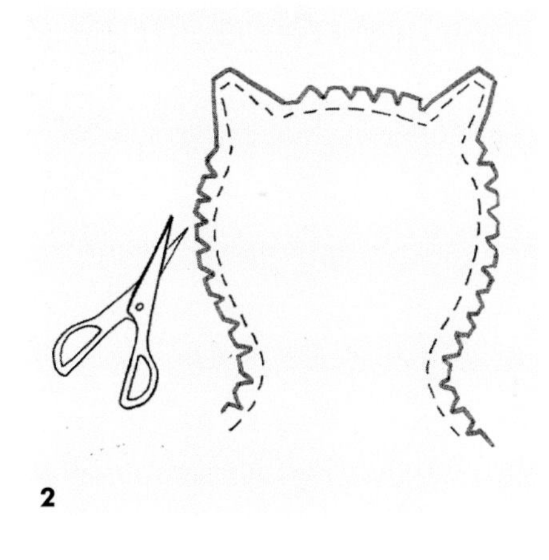

2

3

4

Place pattern pieces on fabric and cut out with care.

1 Place the cat pieces right sides together and pin and tack them together. Sew from A to B, leaving a 3cm (1¼in.) opening under the armpit for turning and stuffing. This pattern is fairly large, so sewing on a machine is very manageable, and also recommended.

2 Clip the curves around the head shape.

3 Turn to the right side, paying extra attention to the ears, which will need to be 'pushed out' with a blunt instrument like a fat knitting needle. Then stuff.

4 Oversew the opening to close it.

5 Add facial features/whiskers.

TO MAKE THE DRESS:

1 Sew the dress pieces together with right sides together to make two side seams, but leaving shoulders open.
2 Sew the lining pieces together in the same way.
3 Turn the dress to the right side and slip the dress inside the lining with the wrong side of the lining facing upwards and the right side of the lining on top of the right side of the dress.
4 Stitch the dress to the lining around the armholes and the neckline.
5 Ease the dress through the shoulders of the lining to turn the dress to the right side with the garment now lined.
6 By hand, slip-stitch together the shoulder seams of both the dress and the lining.

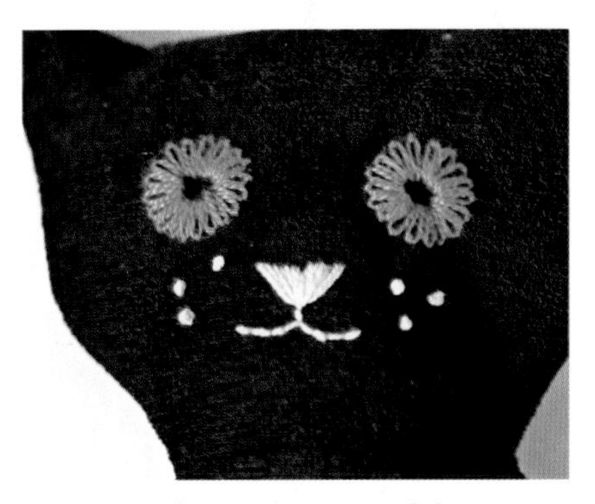

Daisy stitch for the eyes, French knot whiskers and a satin-stitch nose!

Man and lady dolls

These are so cute together, it would be a shame to split them up! Their hair is pom-poms, which makes them a little quirky, but you can do wool hair to make them more traditional. These dolls are small and fiddly. Only experienced sewers would be advised to use a sewing machine to make them, as the corners are tight and accurate sewing is needed. Hand sewing is more controllable, but remember to keep the stitches close together as the dolls will otherwise not be durable.

YOU WILL NEED

FOR BODIES

- 2 doll pieces (per doll; see p.134)
- Stuffing

FOR MAN'S OUTFIT

- 2 shirt pieces (see p.134), one cut in half from the mid neck to the bottom edge
- 2 trouser pieces (see p.134)
- 12cm (4¾in.) narrow elastic

FOR LADY'S OUTFIT

- 2 dress pieces (see p.135)
- 2 frill pieces for the sleeves, 3cm (1¼in.) wide by 18cm long (7in.)
- 2 knicker pieces (see p.134)
- 12cm (4¾in.) narrow elastic

Place pattern pieces on fabric and cut out with care.

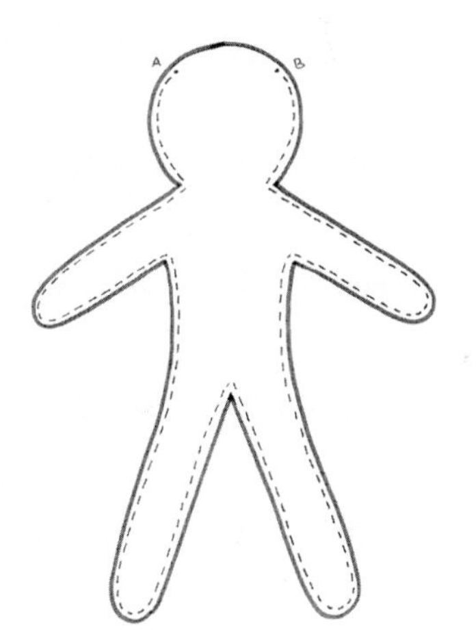

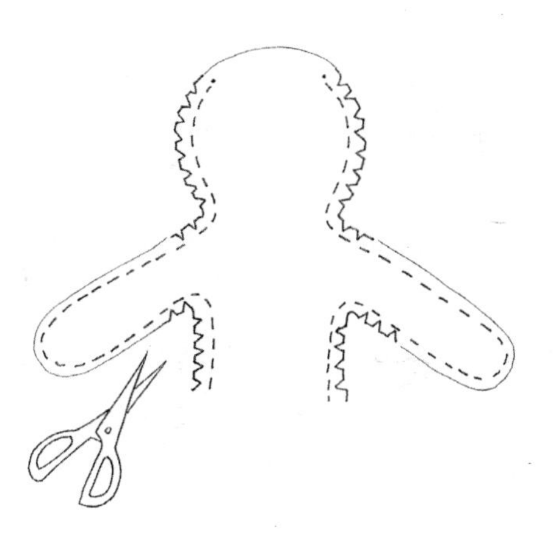

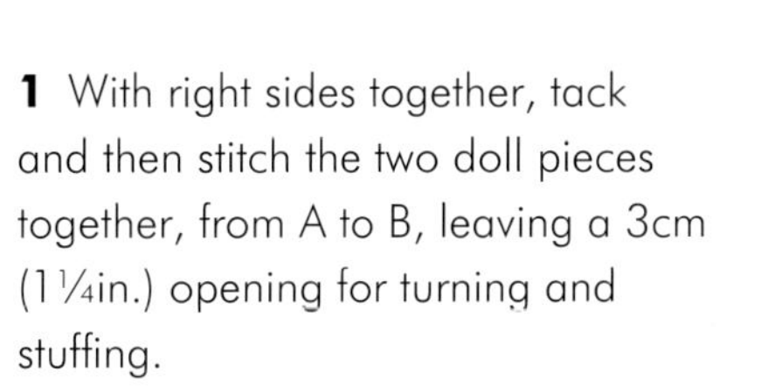

1 With right sides together, tack and then stitch the two doll pieces together, from A to B, leaving a 3cm (1¼in.) opening for turning and stuffing.

2 Clip the curves and turn the doll to the right side.

3 Stuff the doll firmly.

4 Oversew the opening to close.

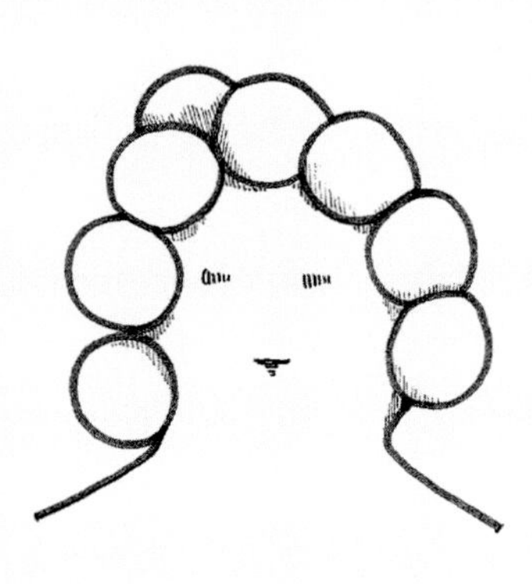

5 Add hair and face – the pom-poms are held in place with tiny stitches and the facial features are satin stitches.

MAN'S OUTFIT

Shirt

1 Stitch the two pieces together, with right sides together, at the shoulder.
2 Add trim to the edge of the sleeve or turn under to make a hem.
3 Stitch the side seams from underarm to hem.
4 Clip the seam on the inside under the arms.
5 Turn under at the back to make a hem and add a fastening – the best choice being a hook and eye or a snap fastener.

Trousers

1 Sew the centre seam.
2 Sew the inside-leg seam.
3 Make a tiny hem at the bottom edge of the trousers.
4 Sew one outside-leg seam
5 Make a narrow facing for the waist.
6 Sew the other outside seam.
7 Use narrow elastic through the casing to bring the trousers in at the waist.

Waistcoat

1 Take two front pieces and one back piece and trim.
2 Sew the shoulders and side seams.
3 Zigzag-stitch from the neck edge or add trim.

LADY'S DRESS

1 Cut one dress piece down the centre from the mid neck to the hem to create two back pieces.
2 Sew shoulders seams.
3 Finish the ruffle with a tiny hem.
4 Finish the neck edge by turning it under to make a hem or by adding trim.
5 Gather the sleeve ruffles to fit the armhole.

6 Sew the side seams and sleeve ruffle in one seam.
7 Add trim.
8 Sew back seam leaving a 3cm (1¼in.) gap at the neck.
9 Finish the opening by turning it back to make a seam, and add a fastening – the best choice being hook and eye or a snap fastener.

Knickers

1 Sew the crotch.
2 Sew the back onto the leg edges.
3 Sew the first side seam.
4 Make a narrow casing at the waist.
5 Sew the second side seam.
6 Thread the elastic through the casing. Knot, and trim ends.

Dolls made by Janine Phillipson.

Painted fabric dolls

You need to be creative to make these dolls, and also to be able to paint! Follow the design shown here or design something unique by drawing your own character and making it into a soft sculpture. These dolls represent different cultures, but you can choose a character from a book or from a different era if you are stuck for ideas.

YOU WILL NEED

- **2 pattern pieces made from the outline of your doll shape**
- **Fabric paint (check the instructions to make sure the paint is suitable for your chosen fabric)**

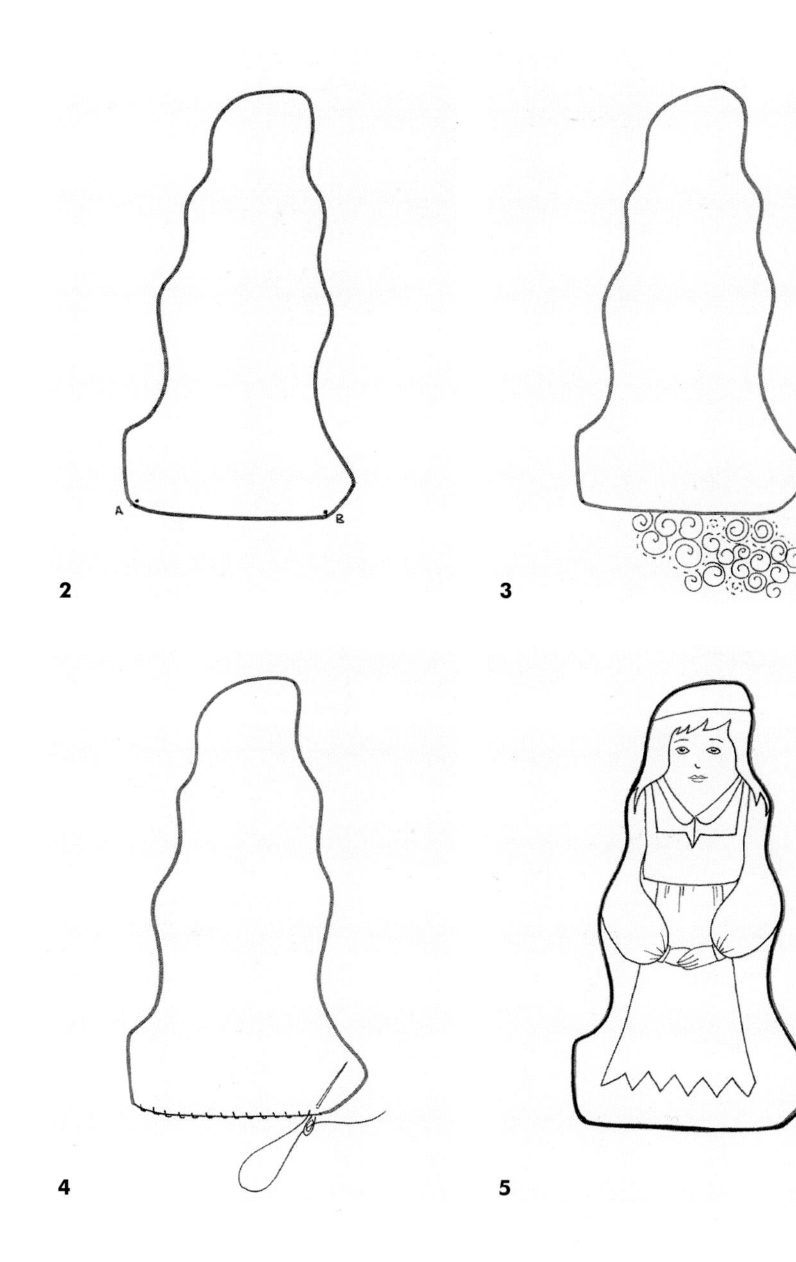

If you have designed and drawn your own doll, create pattern pieces by tracing round the outline of your doll shape and adding a 1cm (3⁄8in.) seam allowance.Place the pattern pieces on the fabric and cut out with care.

1 Place the two doll-shaped pieces with wrong sides together.

2 Oversew the two pieces from A to B, leaving a 3cm (1 1⁄4in.) opening.

3 Stuff firmly, being careful to fill out all the awkward shapes.

4 Oversew to close the opening.

5 Hand-paint your chosen design.

Designed and made by Elysia Wormesley.

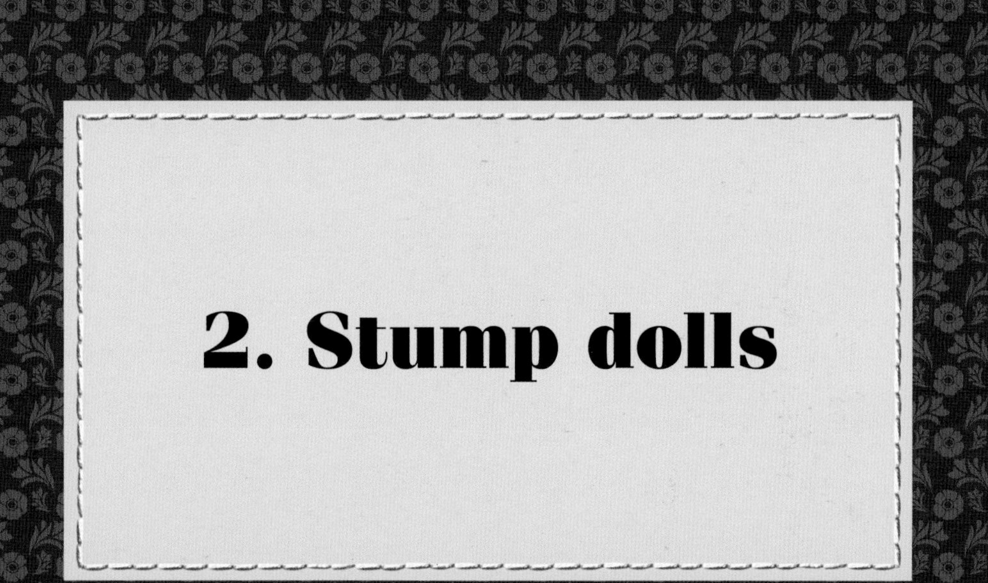

2. Stump dolls

Fairy

This is a stump doll which is made from just one simple shape, and it has no limbs. It is just one piece which becomes the head and body. The fairy also has no head shaping, which makes it look really odd before you add the hair. The placing of the hair creates the shape of the face, so it is really easy and fun to watch this take shape in your hands! This is a simple shape with no corners, so fine to sew on the machine as well as by hand.

YOU WILL NEED

- 2 stump pieces (see p.137)
- 2 strips of fabric, one 11cm (4½in.) by 36cm (14¼in.) for the skirt and the other 16cm (6¼in.) by 5cm (2in.) for the bodice
- 4 wing pieces
- 1 strip of fabric 2.5 x 22cm (1in x 8¾in.) for the arms
- Wool or embroidery silks for hair and sequins for hairband
- 2 pieces of ribbon 2cm (¾in.) long, to become the 'slippers', or feet

Place the pattern pieces on the fabric and cut with care.

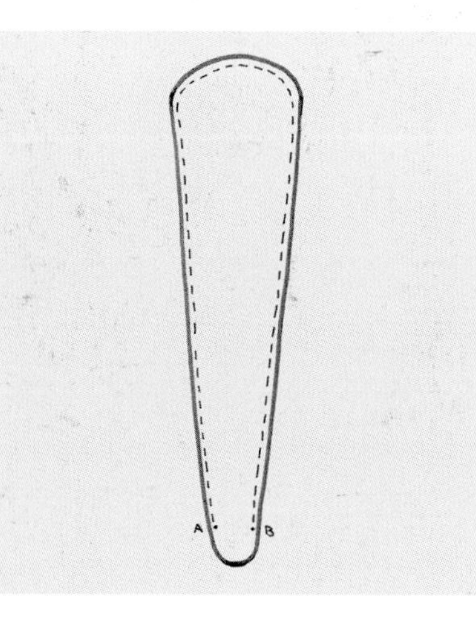

1 With the right sides together, sew from A to B.

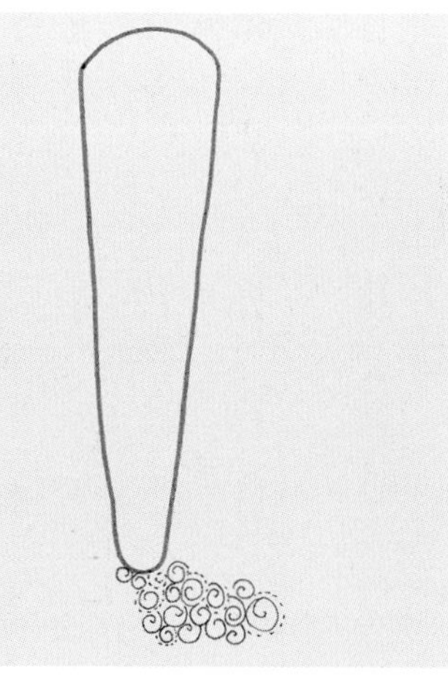

2 Turn to the right side and stuff.

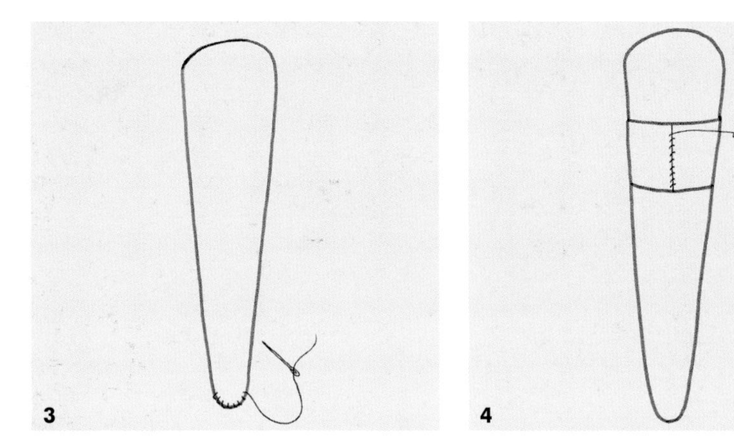

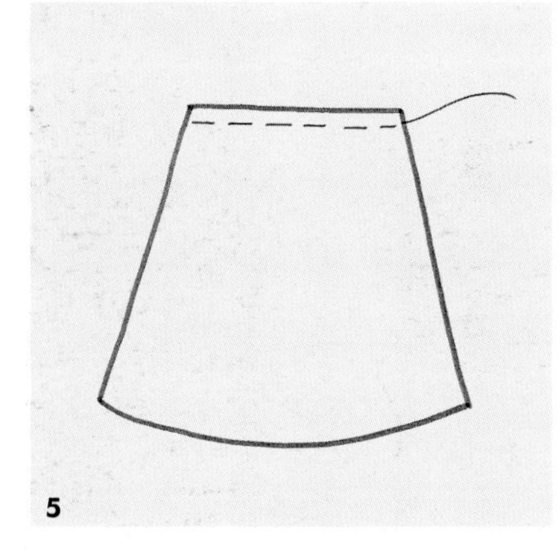

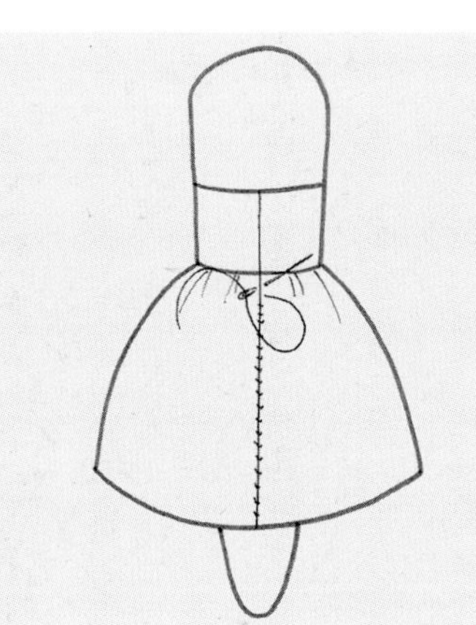

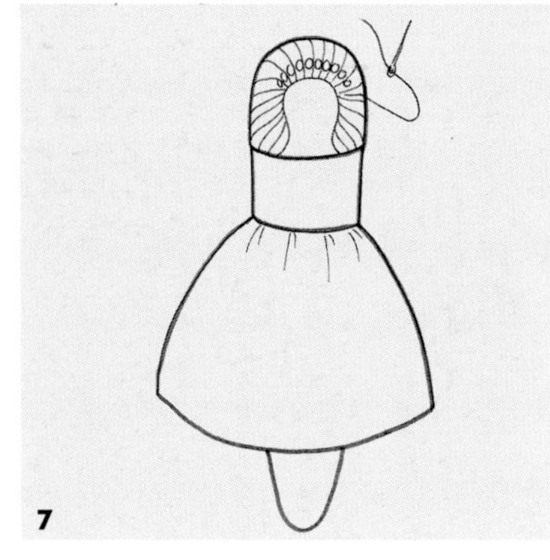

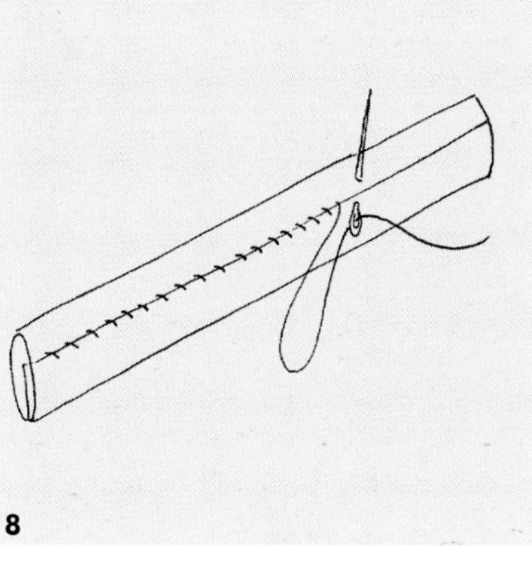

3 Oversew the opening to close.

4 Wrap bodice piece round the 'body' (as indicated on the pattern) and secure with a tiny slip stitch. Turn under the bottom edge by folding up the fabric. Do not sew.

5 Gather the skirt piece to fit the waist and hem the edge.

6 Place the skirt on to the waist. Tuck the gathered edge under the bottom of the bodice, and slip-stitch the folded bodice bottom edge to the skirt to hold the two together. Tack the skirt piece together at the back before creating a seam using tiny running stitches.

7 Create a hairband of sequins on the face area as indicated and sew pieces of wool in long and short stitches all over the head area to make hair.

8 With the right sides together sew a seam along the strip at one edge and turn through to create a narrow strip which will become the arms. Turn to the right side. Using a pressing cloth, gently press so that the strip is flat but does not have a crease.

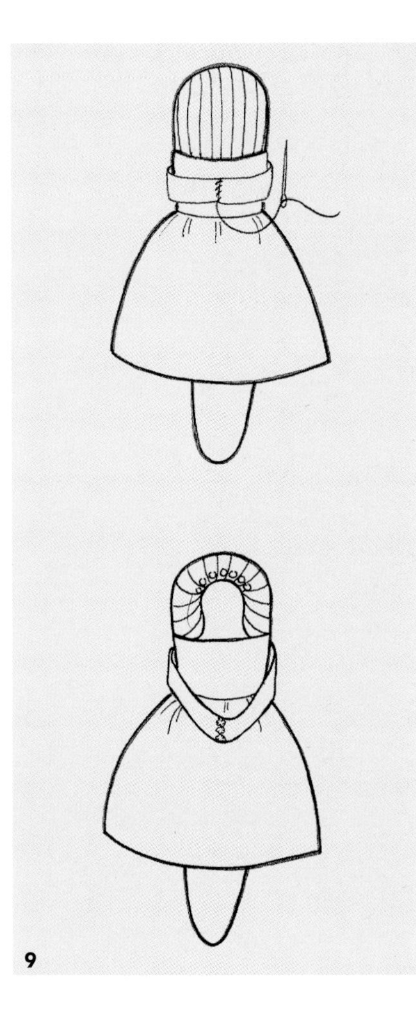

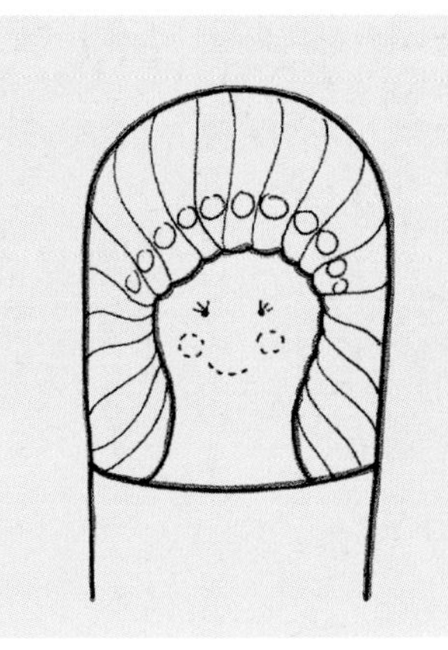

9 Secure the arm strip at the back of the bodice and bring the two edges to the front of the doll, slip-stitching them together where they meet, and adding a trim to look like a bracelet on one newly formed arm.

10 Add hand-embroidery stitches to make the face.

11 With tiny stitches secure the two pieces of ribbon to form ballet slippers on the feet.

12 Zigzag-stitch the edges of the wings and secure the finished wings at the centre of the bodice at the back. For neatness cover with a folded strip of bodice fabric.

Doll with a dolly in her pocket

This 'stump' has a shaped head but no arms or legs. Its shape makes it suitable to be made on the sewing machine, if you have one, as there are no fiddly corners. Make both the dolls in the same way; the bunny, however, needs to be sewn wrong sides together, by oversewing it or using a blanket stitch for a neat finish, sandwiching the ears in between the two layers.

YOU WILL NEED

- 2 doll pieces (see p.138)
- 1 pocket piece
- Ribbon for a larger doll's pocket to make it into an apron
- Felt for facial features and bunny
- Wool for hair

Place the pattern pieces on fabric and cut them out with care. If you want to use a plain fabric for the face, cut the pattern into two pieces across the narrowest part – the 'neck' – and cut the face and body from different fabrics.

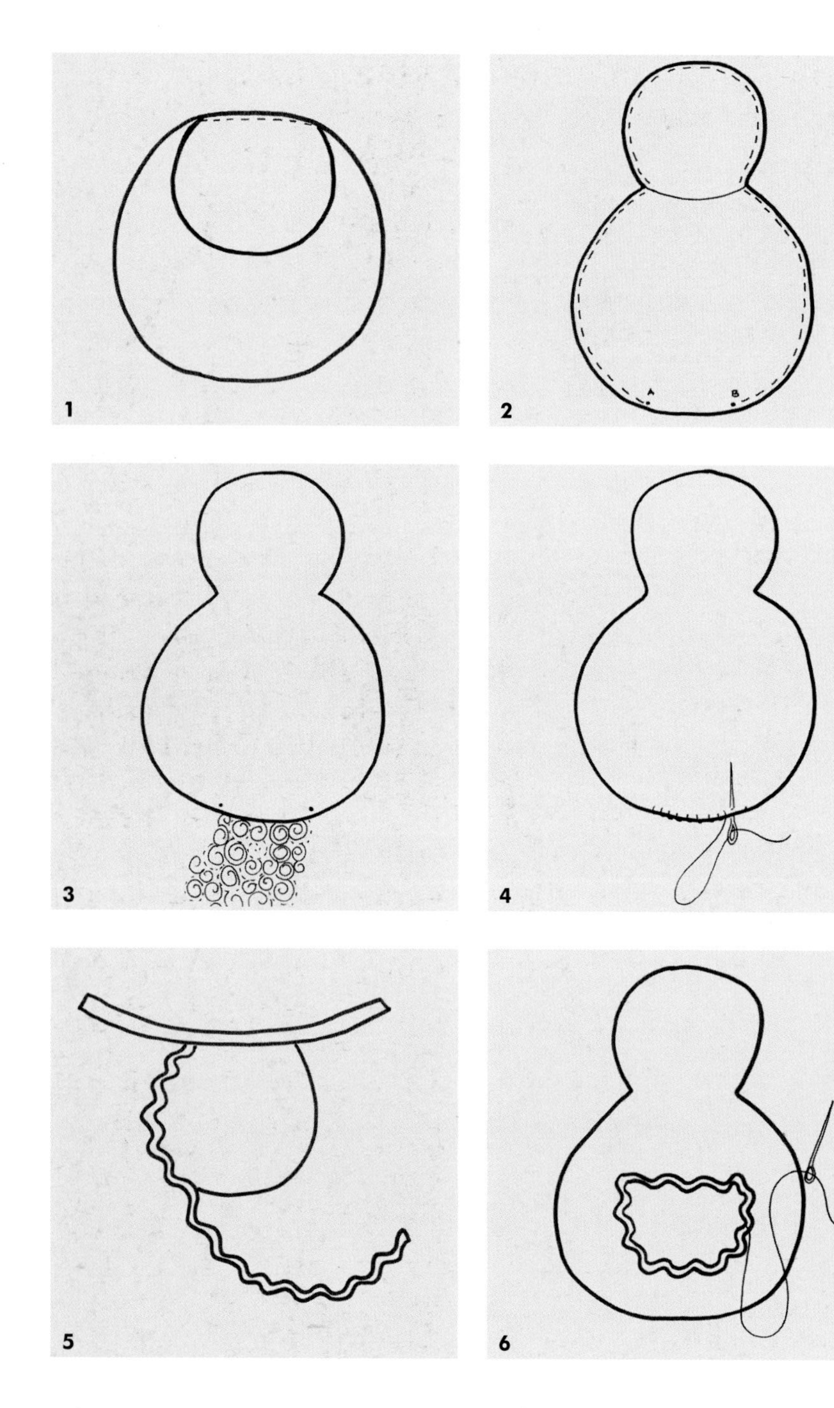

1 If you are choosing a plain 'skin' coloured fabric and a patterned fabric for the body or 'dress', first place the head part with the right side touching the body as shown. Make a seam to join the head to the body, on both front and back pieces. Repeat this for the small doll if you are making both in the same way. Press the seam open before bringing the 'head' into its position.

2 Working with the head and body now as one piece, with right sides together sew from A to B leaving a 3cm (1¼in) opening for turning and stuffing.

3 Turn to the right side and stuff.

4 Oversew the opening to close.

5 Turn the hem under for the apron and add ric rac ribbon trim to the edge. Attach ribbon with a straight stitch at the top of the apron. Prepare the pocket for the smaller doll by stitching ric rac to the top edge only, to neaten the edge.

6 For the small doll, hand-stitch the pocket to the doll body using ric rac, which hides the edge of the pocket fabric. Use lots of tiny stitches to make this strong enough to hold the bunny.

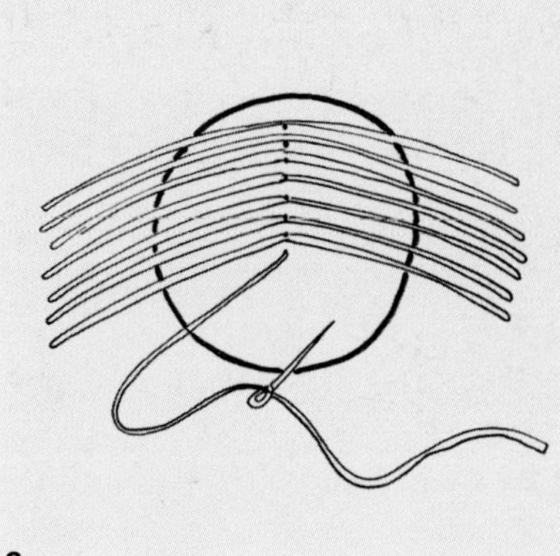

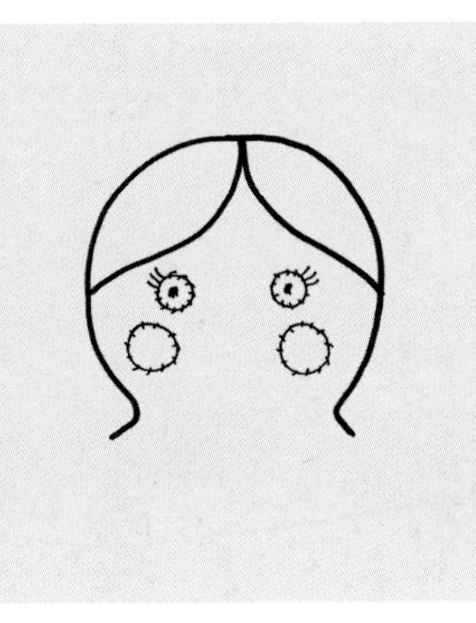

11

7 For the big doll's hair, if a bun is desired make a circular cushion of felt and attach it to the back of the head. Make this is as big or small as you like. Stitch the bun to cover it in wool hair, from the edge to the centre working round the edge of the circular shape, and going to the same centre point with each stitch you make. A felt 'fringe' shape is made in the same way and covered in wool 'hair' before being attached with a hand stitch.

8 For the little doll's hair, cut lengths of wool and drape them over the back of the head. Couch the wool onto the head with a central stitch, then gather into two bunches.

9 Attach the collar with hand stitches.

10 Add felt eyes and cheeks.

11 For the bunny, place the pieces wrong sides together and oversew them together, leaving a gap into which you need to 'poke' the ears before carefully stitching them in place. The eyes are French knots.

Doll designed and made by Charlotte Ladner.

Topsy-turvy doll

This is a stump doll with head and arm shapes, and the expectation is that the legs are under the skirt. In fact under the skirt is another head and arms, hence the name of the doll!

These are popular with children – I had one which was Little Red Riding Hood at one end and the wolf at the other. I was reminded of these dolls by the one shown here, bought on the beach in Barbados and wearing two flamboyant outfits.

This one is young and vibrant at one end – I was tempted to give her a baby to hold – and old, but glamorous at the other, wearing a skirt covered in lace from days gone by. You can dress the dolls any way you like and add your own surprises! This doll, being small, is a very fiddly shape, and for that reason you should not attempt to make it on the sewing machine.

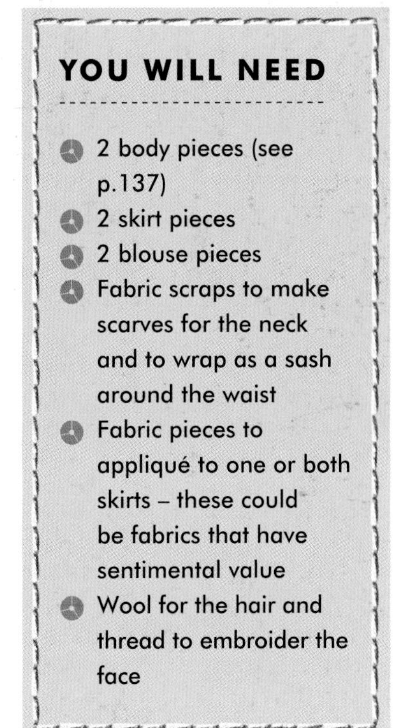

YOU WILL NEED

- 2 body pieces (see p.137)
- 2 skirt pieces
- 2 blouse pieces
- Fabric scraps to make scarves for the neck and to wrap as a sash around the waist
- Fabric pieces to appliqué to one or both skirts – these could be fabrics that have sentimental value
- Wool for the hair and thread to embroider the face

Place the pattern pieces on the fabric and cut out with care.

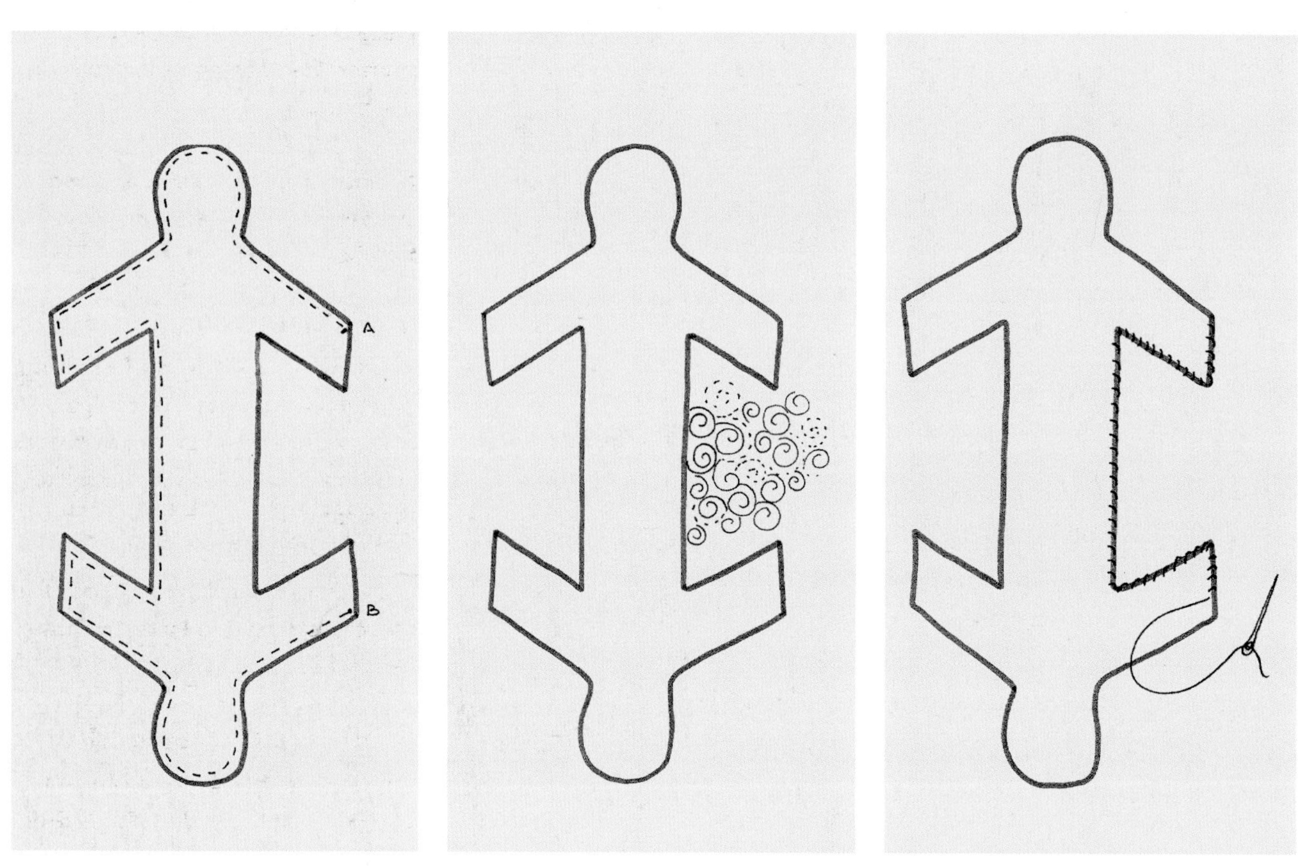

1 With the right sides together and using a close-together running stitch or a back stitch for strength, sew from A to B leaving an opening as shown.

2 Turn to the right side, pushing the seams out with either a blunt knitting needle or a rounded spoon handle, and stuff firmly.

3 Oversew the underarm area to close the seam.

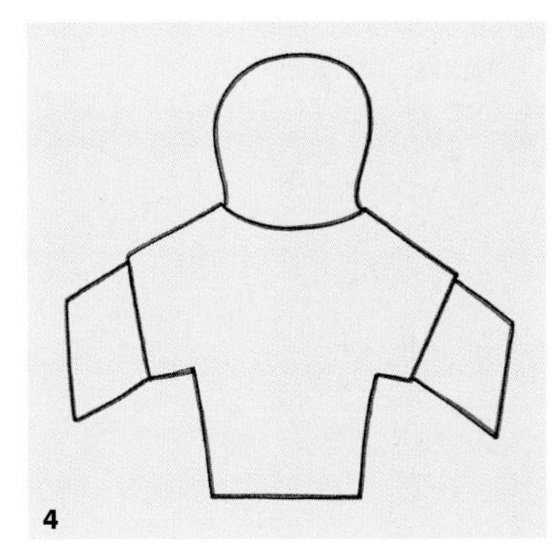

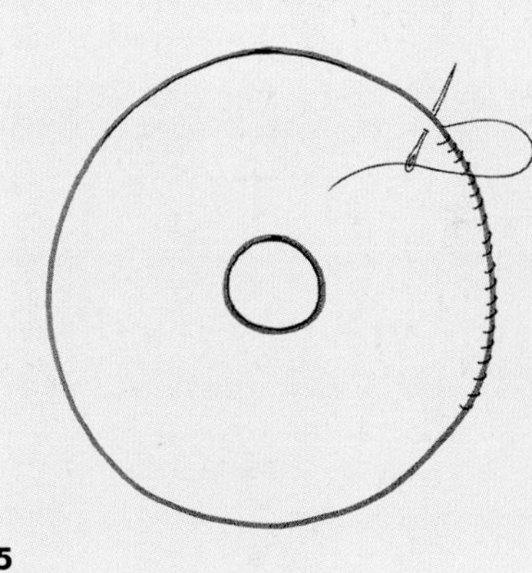

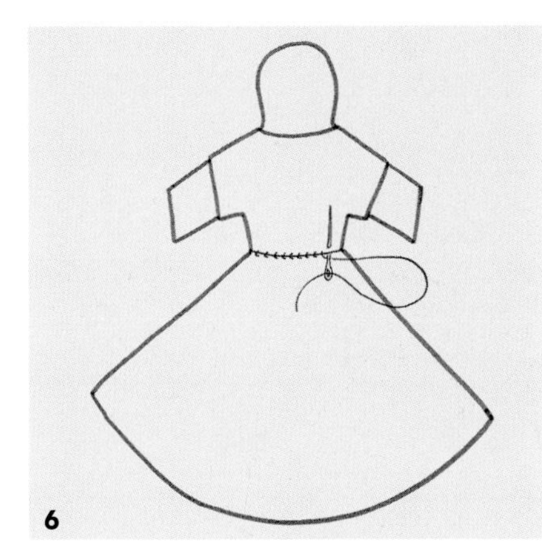

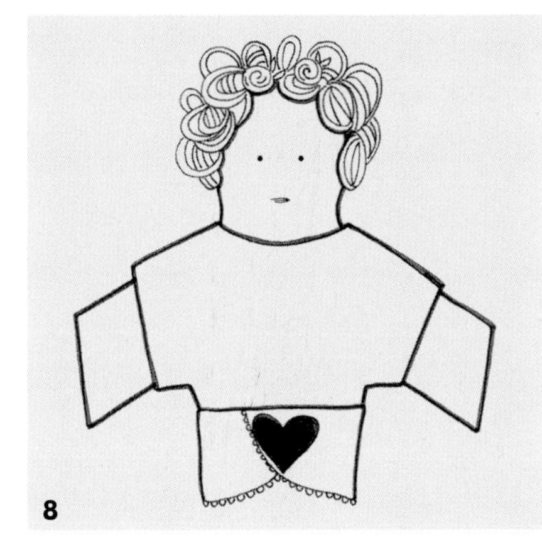

4 On both ends place the blouse piece over the head shape and oversew the underarm seam to keep it in place.

5 Place the two skirt pieces wrong sides together and slip-stitch them together by hand.

Alternatively, place them right sides together and sew together by making a narrow seam close to the edge, being sure to keep the circular shape. This is tricky, which is why I used the slip stitch.

6 Use tiny hand stitches to attach the skirt on both sides to the body of the doll.

7 Cover the stitched seam with a wrap-around fabric sash. Neck ties or headscarves can also be wrapped into position later.

8 Create the hair from curls of wool secured with hand stitches. The facial features are embroidered onto the face to complete the doll.

3. Dolls to knit and crochet

These instructions are for knitters and those who can crochet already – they will be hard to follow if you are not already used to working from a pattern! There are many good books available to teach you how to follow a pattern.

CROCHET ABBREVIATIONS

*	asterisks indicate that the sequence described between the asterisks is repeated. The number of repeats required is stated.
ch1	chain one stitch
dc	double crochet
dc2tog	double crochet two together (see box opposite)

dc2tog: To double crochet two stitches together, insert the crochet hook into the next stitch, wind the yarn around the hook and draw it through. Insert the hook into the next stitch, and again wind yarn round the hook and draw it through. Wind yarn around the hook and now draw it through all three stitches on the hook. You have made a double crochet decrease!

KNITTING ABBREVIATIONS

*	asterisks indicate that the sequence described between the asterisks is repeated. The number of repeats required is stated.
dec1	decrease one stitch
inc1	increase one stitch by knitting into the front and back of that stitch
k	knit
k2tog	knit two stitches together to decrease a stitch
m1	make one stitch (see box)
MS	main shade (colour) of the yarn
p	purl
p2tog	purl two stitches together to decrease a stitch
sl1	slip one stitch
st	stitch
st st	stocking stitch
yfwd	bring yarn forward as if to make the next stitch

At the start of each pattern the suggested tension and the finished size of the doll is given.

TIP *when crocheting 'in the round', it will help if you place a marker or a piece of contrasting thread where you finish each row, to indicate the row end. Move the marker up as you work each row.*

m1: To make one stitch, pick up the horizontal strand of yarn between the stitch just knitted and the next stitch, then knit into the back of it.

Flat bunny doll

This bunny has a knitted head, crocheted arms and legs and a body made from fabric. To make this doll you will need to be able to knit, crochet and sew, and have experience of shaping. Have fun finding fabric you like (small prints work particularly well) and choose colours of wool (for the head and limbs) to complement it.

YOU WILL NEED

- 1 x 50g (1¾oz) ball Rowan Cashsoft DK (shade 501, lilac) (main shade)
- 1 x 50g (1¾oz) ball Rowan Cashsoft 4-ply in contrasting shade for legs/arms (shade 446)
- Needles: 3mm (US size 2)
- Hooks: 3.50mm (US size 4) and 3.00mm (US size 2)
- 20 x 30cm (8 x 12in.) piece of vintage-style fabric for the dress
- Small piece of muslin for the face
- A little wadding for the filling
- Embroidery thread for the face

Tension: Not crucial.

Finished size: 42cm(16½in.)

Head (knitted)

Using MS, cast on 14 sts with 3.25mm (US 3) needles.
St st four rows.

Shape neck

k2tog, knit to end of row.
p2tog, purl to end of row.
Repeat these two rows, three times – eight sts.
st st for two rows.

Increase for head

inc1 at end of each end of the next knit row.
Purl one row.
Repeat last two rows, three times – 16 sts.

Next increase row

inc1, *k3 sts, m1*.
Repeat this three times, k2, inc1 in last st – 22 sts.
St st for five rows, starting and ending with a purl row.
Inc in first st and in last st – 24 sts place marker at end of row.
st st for 15 rows, starting and ending with a purl row.

Shape top of head

dec1 at each end of the next four rows – 16 sts.
k2tog across row – 8 sts.
Purl one row.
k2tog across row – 4 sts.
Break yarn leaving a fairly long tail, then thread through the remaining stitches and secure.

Make another head piece to match.

Ears

Using 3mm hook and MS, ch2.

4dc into first st (place marker to indicate the end of row).
2dc into next dc, 1dc into next st repeat once more – 6dc.
Continue to inc 2dc each round evenly spaced, until you have 16dc.

Continue to dc straight for another 14 rows. Fasten off.

Making up the head

1 Gently press the head pieces using a damp cloth.
2 With wrong sides together and using a small back stitch, sew the head together, leaving the neck open.
3 Stuff lightly.
4 Pinch the bottom of the ears as per photograph on p.45, and sew carefully to the top of the head.

Arms

Using contrsting shade and 3.5mm hook, ch2.

6dc into 2nd chain from hook.
2dc into each dc – 12 sts.
2dc then 2dc into next st repeat three more times – 16 sts.
dc four rows.
dc2tog, dc into next 6dc repeat once – 14 sts.
Work one row straight, changing yarn to MS in last stitch.
*dc2tog, dc into next 5dc * repeat once – 12 sts.
dc one row.
dc one row.
dc2tog, dc into next 4dc repeat once more – ten sts.

Continue these ten sts for ten rows, stuffing very lightly as you go.
Fasten off and secure.
Make another arm to match.

Legs

Using contrasting shade and 3.5mm hook (US 4/E), ch2.
6dc into second chain.
2dc into each stitch – 12 sts.

1dc, 2dc into next st, then repeat six times (18 sts).
1dc into each st.
2dc into 1st st, dc into next 5dc, repeat once (20 sts).
Work three rows dc.
Work one row dc, changing yarn to MS in last stitch.
Work one row dc (changing yarn back to contrasting shade in last st).
Continue dc in spiral rounds for another eight rows.

Stuff the bottom of the leg very lightly.

dc2tog, dc into next 6dc repeat once – 14 sts.
Work one row dc.
dc2tog, dc into next 5dc, repeat once – 12 sts.
Continue straight in dc for another ten rows. Fasten off.

Dress

1 Trace off the pattern for the dress of the long-legged doll on p.136. Use it at the same size as it is printed in the book (i.e. there is no need to enlarge this pattern piece on a photocopier). Use this to cut two pieces from the fabric, for front and back.
2 With wrong sides together, sandwich the legs and arms carefully inside the dress and sew round, leaving the neck open.
3 Turn right side out, so that legs and arms pop out into position. Stuff lightly.
4 Add a pocket or other decorative detail as desired.
5 Turning over the neckline of the dress, insert the knitted neck of the bunny and carefully stitch into place.

Designed and made by Roz Esposito. Wool by Rowan.

Crocheted bunnies

These are for the maker with some experience, but are fairly easy to do. The bunnies are crocheted in a spiral fashion, so it is helpful to use a marker to show the beginning of each round. They look cute in a pair, and the cream and brown look especially good together!

YOU WILL NEED

FOR THE BODIES:

- 1 x 50g (1¾oz) Rowan Alpaca (shade 205, cream)
- 1 x 50g (1¾oz) Rowan Alpaca Tangier (shade 213, brown)
- Hook: 3.5mm (US size 4)
- 2 pairs of toys' eyes

Tension: not critical, as long as the dc is tight enough that the stuffing doesn't show through.

Finished size: 47cm (18½in.)

Ears, head and body

ch3.
6dc in first st.
2dc in next st, 1dc in next st around – 9dc.
2dc in every third st – 12dc.

Working on these 12dc, work in a spiral fashion for 40 rows or until the ear is 17cm (6¾in.).
Finish off.

Make another ear the same, but do not finish off.
ch3, then crochet around the first ear, so joining the two ears.
dc into each of the 3 chain, then around the second ear – 26dc.
dc along the other side of the 3 chain and around the ear.

Continue in dc for around 50 rows or 20cm (8in.) long from the top of ears until ears and body measure 20cm (7¾in.).
Finish off.

Arms

Start with the hand. ch3.
6dc into first chain.
2dc into each chain.
2dc in the fourth chain – 15dc.
Continue three rows straight.
Next row dec for arm: dc2tog, dc into next 3dc.
Repeat 3 times – 12dc.
dc2tog. dc into next 4dc.
Repeat twice – 10dc.

Stuff hand lightly.
Continue these 10dc until arm measures 12cm (4¾in.) each.
Stuff lightly.

Make another the same.

Legs

ch3.
6dc into first chain.
2dc into each chain – 12dc.
Increase two sts evenly on next row – 14 sts.
Work four rows straight.
dec2 evenly – 12 sts.
Work four rows straight.
Fasten off.

Make another the same.

Making up

1 Stuff the ears lightly.
2 Attach eyes and sew eyelashes with cotton for girl bunny.
3 Sew a pink cross for the mouth.
4 Stuff the head lightly. Pinch in the sides of the head to create a neck.
5 Fasten with a few small stitches.
6 Stuff the remaining body.
7 Stuff the legs and sew neatly around at the bottom.
8 Sew on the arms just under the neck.

Dress for girl bunny

Using shade A (see box, right), ch35 and join with a slip stitch to create a ring, being careful not to twist the chain.

ch1.
dc into each chain around – 34dc.
Join with a slip stitch to the beginning of the round, while changing colour to shade B.
ch1.
dc into next 6dc.
ch5 for armhole.
Miss 5dc.
dc into next 12dc.
ch5.
Miss 5dc.
dc into remaining 6dc.
Join with a slip stitch.
dc into next 6dc.
6dc into 5 chain.
2dc into the next dc.
dc in the next 10dc.
2dc into next dc.
6dc into 5 chain.
6dc.
Join with a slip stitch, changing colour to shade C (38dc).
ch1.
dc all around.
Join with a slip stitch.

YOU WILL NEED

FOR THE DRESS:

- 1 x 50g (1¾oz) Rowan Alpaca DK (shade 214, spring leaf) (shade A)
- 1 x 50g (1¾oz) Rowan Alpaca DK Lagoon (shade 210, light blue) (shade B)
- 1 x 50g (1¾oz) Rowan Cashsoft DK in pink (shade C)
- Hook: 3.5mm (US size 4)

*Repeat the round, changing colours every two rows as set for 18 rows.

Work one row in shade A then finish with a row of picot as follows:
ch1.
2dc.
ch3.
Slip stitch into same st.
dc3, ch3, slip stitch into same st.
Continue all the way round.
Fasten off.
Weave in all ends.
Press lightly under a damp tea towel.

Vest for boy bunny

Cast on 28 sts.
k1, p1.
p1, k1.
This forms the pattern.
Repeat last two rows four times more.
Repeat first row again.
k1.
yfwd.
k2tog.
p1.
k1 to end.
Continue in moss st for another three rows.

Shaping the armholes

p1.
k1 for six sts.
Cast off next 4 sts (for armhole).
Moss st eight sts (for back).
Cast off next four sts (for armhole).
Moss st for remaining six sts (for front).
Working each piece separately, continue on the last six sts.
Moss st for six rows.
Cast off in moss st.
With WS facing, complete back with moss st for six rows.
Finish as front.
Last front piece, with WS facing, moss st for six rows and finish as before.

Making up

1 Neatly sew in loose ends.
2 Join armholes with just a few stitches at the top of each side.
3 Sew on the button opposite the buttonhole. If you prefer, fasten down the 'collar' with a few stitches.

Designed and made by Roz Esposito. Wool by Rowan.

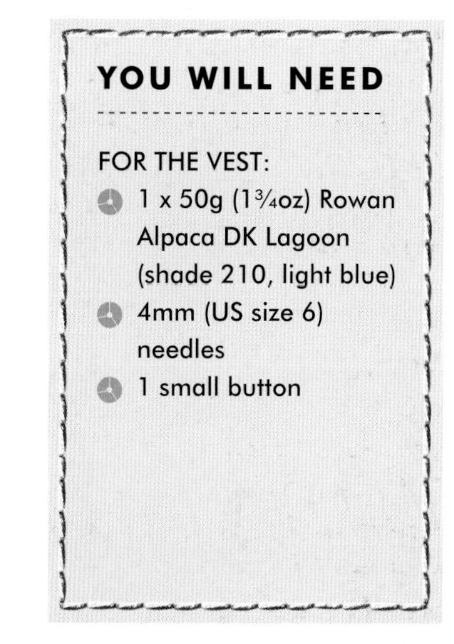

YOU WILL NEED

FOR THE VEST:
- 1 x 50g (1¾oz) Rowan Alpaca DK Lagoon (shade 210, light blue)
- 4mm (US size 6) needles
- 1 small button

Knitted doll

This 'hippie chick' is made from luxury yarn, which makes her extra special! She is for the knitter who has a little experience of shaping. The crown, flower and shoes are all crocheted.

Body

Head

Cast on 22 sts and work in st st for 42 rows.

Make two.

Shape shoulders

Cast off 2 sts at the beginning of the next four rows (14 sts).

*k2tog then knit to end of row.

p2tog* then purl to end of row.

Repeat these two rows twice more – eight sts.

Neck

St st for two rows.

Increase for head

inc 1 st at each end of row.

p1.

Repeat these two rows three more times – 16 sts.

Next row

inc in first st.

*k3 sts.

m1*.

Repeat sequence between asterisks three more times.

k2.

inc in last st – 22 sts.

st st for five rows; starting and ending with a purl row.

Next row

inc in first st, knit to end of row, inc in last st – 24 sts.

Place marker at end of row to help count rows.

st st for 15 rows, starting and ending with a purl row.

YOU WILL NEED

FOR THE BODY:

- 1 x 50g (1¾oz) Rowan Classic Baby Alpaca DK
- 1 x 50g (1¾oz) chunky yarn for hair
- 2 small buttons for eyes
- scrap of red felt for mouth
- a little stuffing
- 3.25mm knitting needles (US size 3)

Tension: not critical, but 26sts x 30 rows 10cm (4in.) when using 3.25mm (US size 3) needles

Finished size: 55cm (21¾in.) high

Shape top of head.
dec1 at each end of next four rows – 16 sts.
k2tog across row – eight sts.
Purl one row.
k2tog across row – four sts.
Cut yarn leaving a long tail, thread through remaining stitches and fasten off.

Legs

Cast on ten sts.
st st for 27cm (10½in.)
k2tog across row – five sts.
p2tog.
p1.
Cut yarn leaving enough to thread through remaining stitches and fasten off. The legs can either be left to 'roll' into a long tube, or sewn gently at the back.

Arms

Cast on eight sts.
st st for 12cm (4¾in.).
k2tog – four sts.
p2tog – two sts.
Finish as for the legs.

Making up

1 Gently press body pieces under a damp tea towel. Sew up body (with right sides pinned together) using a small back stitch.
2 Turn inside out and stuff lightly.
3 Attach legs at bottom of body, and arms at shoulders.
4 Using photograph as a guide, sew buttons in place as eyes, sewing a few eyelashes at each side.
5 Cut out a small heart-shaped smile out of the red felt, and sew into place.
6 Cut long strands of chunky wool for the hair, adding an extra inch to allow for trimming later. Taking a small bunch at a time, secure to the head using a long back stitch.
7 Finish off securely. Trim hair.
8 Adorn and decorate as you please!

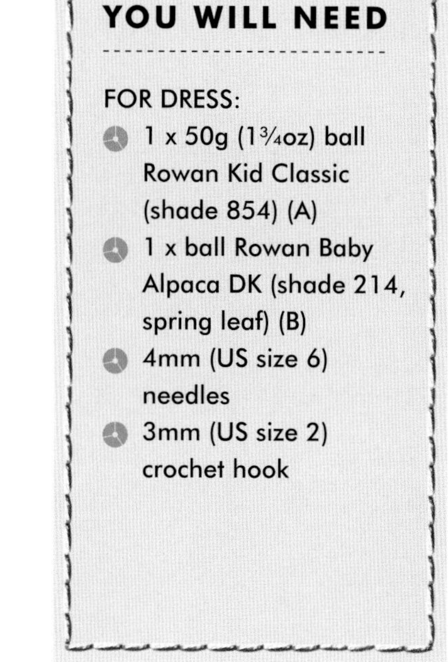

YOU WILL NEED

FOR DRESS:
- 1 x 50g (1¾oz) ball Rowan Kid Classic (shade 854) (A)
- 1 x ball Rowan Baby Alpaca DK (shade 214, spring leaf) (B)
- 4mm (US size 6) needles
- 3mm (US size 2) crochet hook

Dress

(Front and back alike.)
With 4mm (US size 6) needles and yarn A, cast on 60 sts and st st two rows.
k2tog across row – 30 sts.
Purl 1 row.
Change to yarn B.
st st for 25 rows, starting and ending with a purl row.

Next row

k5, k2tog repeat across row, ending with k2 (26 sts).
Purl one row.

Armhole shaping

k2.
k2tog.
k to last four sts.
k2tog.
k2 – 24 sts.
Purl one row.
k2.
k2tog.
*k4.
k2tog* three times.
k2 – 20 sts.
st st three rows.
k2.
k2tog.
Knit to last four sts.
k2tog.
k2 – 18 sts.

Purl one row.
Change to yarn A.
Knit one row.
Cast off.

Making up

1 Press each piece very lightly under a tea towel, and with right sides together, sew each side of the dress to the armhole.
2 Sew a few stitches each side of the neck, leaving a gap wide enough for a doll's head to go through.
3 Turn the right way round.
4 Using 3mm hook and yarn A, dc neatly all around the armhole.

Shoes (crocheted)

ch2.
6dc into 2nd chain from hook.
2dc in each chain – 12 sts.
dc7 rows.
Don't fasten off.
Chain 35, then fasten off.
Weave in end.
Join yarn to the opposite side of the shoe and ch35. Fasten as before.
Make another shoe.
Use the chains to wind around the doll's leg and tie into a bow.

Crown (crocheted)

ch57.

2 treble in fourth ch from hook.
Make a picot by making 3ch and slip stitch into the side of last treble worked, then treble 2, all in the same stitch.
Miss two sts, 1dc into next st, then miss two sts.
*2 treble, 1 picot and 2 treble all in next stitch.
Miss next two sts.
1dc into next st.
Miss next two sts. *
Repeat from * to * across row finishing on 1dc at end of row.
(Nine fans with picot top.)

Making up

Join the edges to create a crown and stitch neatly to the head.

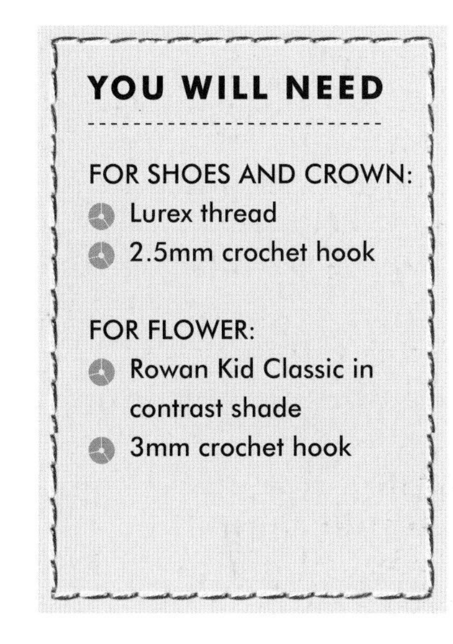

YOU WILL NEED

FOR SHOES AND CROWN:
- Lurex thread
- 2.5mm crochet hook

FOR FLOWER:
- Rowan Kid Classic in contrast shade
- 3mm crochet hook

Flower (crocheted)

ch8.
Close ring with a slip stitch.
ch1.
15dc into ring.
Join with a slip stitch.
*ch2, 2 treble into next st.
ch2.
1dc into next st.
Repeat from * all round. Fasten off.
Sew onto the bottom of the dress.

Designed and made by Roz Esposito. Wool by Rowan.

Worry dolls

Worry dolls are a Central American tradition. When a child has a problem, they tell their worry doll about it, then put the doll under their pillow, and the doll does their worrying for them. This knitting pattern is simple enough that a beginner can make it – or even a child. It is a good way of using up left-over yarn, and the features can be made in a variety of ways.

YOU WILL NEED

- 1 pair of knitting needles, ideally 4 or 4.5mm (US size 6 or 7)
- Odd bits of yarn in different colours
- If using chunky yarn, use one strand; or for sock yarn (or sport weight) use four strands

Tension: None
Size: 15cm (6in.)

Cast on five stitches in the colour you want for the face.

1 k5.
2 p5.
3 k1, inc 1, k3, inc 1, k1 – seven sts.
4 p7.
5 k76, p7.
7 k7.
8 p7.
9 k1, k2tog, k1, k2tog, k1 – five sts.
10 p5.

Now change colour for the body. Tie the two colours together very close to the needle, and leave a long strand of each colour outside the knitting.

11 k5.
12 p5.
13 k1, inc 1, k3, inc1, k1 – seven sts.
14 p7.
15–30 Work 16 rows in st st, starting with a knit row.
31 k1, k2tog, k1, k2tog, k1 – five sts.
32 p5.
33 k5.
34 p5.
35 k1, inc1, k3, inc1, k1.
36 p7.
37–52 Work 16 rows in st st, starting with a knit row.
53 k1, k2tog, k1, k2tog, k1.
54 p5.

Now change back to the face colour.

55 k5.
56 p5.
57 k1, inc1, k3, inc1, k1.
58 p7.
59 k7.
60 p7.
61 k7.
62 p7.
63 k1, k2tog, k1, k2 tog, k1.
64 p5.

Cast off.

Making up

1 Now sew the doll up. You want to have the smooth surface on the outside, but it's easier to sew together inside out, so look at the more bobbly side. First of all, just sew up the body.
2 Now put features on the face. You can use buttons or sequins, or sew different-coloured yarn on using a large-eyed tapestry needle. I've just done eyes and mouth, but the possibilities are endless!
3 Now sew up the head. It's easier to do this the right way round.
4 Finally, sew on the hair. Sew once into the head, and the second time leave a long loop. It's essential to do at least one stitch between each loop, to keep the hair secure. When you've finished, simply cut the loops, so that they form one strand of hair. The hairstyle is up to you, and you could of course sew a hat shape instead, or even leave them bald.

You now have a completed worry doll to help you in times of trouble!

Designed and made by Alex Black.

Mermaid

This is for the maker who enjoys combining their skills of knitting and crochet. It is suitable for someone who has some experience in shaping. The tail and fins are crocheted, and the head, body and arms are knitted. Add a floral crocheted bikini and adorn the mermaid's curly seaweed hair with buttons and shells to add to her magical charm!

YOU WILL NEED

- 1 x 50g (1¾oz) ribbon tape yarn in blue for tail and fins
- 1 x Rowan Cashsoft DK in pale pink for head, body and arms
- 1 x 50g (1¾oz) bouclé yarn in blues/greens for hair
- Small amounts yarn for waist trim and flower bikini
- 1 x pair of small toy's eyes
- Stuffing
- 3.5mm hook
- 4mm hook
- 3.75mm (US size 5) needles (3.5mm/US size 4 would also work)

Tension: Not really critical, so long as dc is tight so that the stuffing doesn't show through.

Size: 34cm (13½in.)

Tail (crocheted)

4mm hook and ribbon tape yarn.

1 ch2, 6dc into first ch.
2 Work 1dc in each dc around.
3 inc2 sts evenly (8dc).
4 Work 1dc in each dc around.
5 inc2 sts evenly – ten sts.
6–11 Repeat last row until there are 22 sts.
12 Work 1dc in each dc around.
13–22 Repeat previous row.
Fasten off.

Tail fins (crocheted)

Make two fins.

1 ch2, 6dc into first chain.
2 Work 1dc in each dc around.
3 inc2 evenly – eight sts.
4 Work 1dc in each dc around.
5 inc2 evenly – ten sts.
6 inc2 evenly – 12 sts.
7 inc2 evenly – 14 sts.
8 Work 1dc in each dc around.
9 dec2 evenly along row – 12 sts.
10 dec2 evenly along row – ten sts.
11 Repeat row 9 – eight sts.
12 Repeat row 9 – six sts.

Fasten off, leaving a long piece of

yarn to use for sewing the fin onto the bottom of the tail.

Stuff the tail lightly, but leave the fins unstuffed.

Head and body (knitted)

Cast on 18 sts.

1–18 Beginning with a knit row, st st for 18 rows ending with a purl row.
19 k2tog. k to last two sts, k2tog – 16 sts.
20 p2tog. p to last two sts. p2tog – 14 sts.
21–24 Repeat last two rows twice more – six sts.

Neck

25 Knit 1 row.
26 Purl 1 row.

Increase for head

27 *inc1, knit to last two sts, inc in last st* – eight sts.
28 *inc1, purl to last two sts, inc in last st* – ten sts.
29–30 Repeat last two rows once more.
31 *inc1, knit to last two sts, inc in last st* – eight sts.
32 Purl one row.

Next row

33 Inc in first st. k4, m1, k5, m1, k5 inc in last st – 20 sts.
Place marker.
34–51 st st for 17 rows, starting and ending with a purl row.

Shape the top of the head

52 dec1 at each end of row – 18 sts.
53–55 Repeat the last row three times.
56 k2tog across row – six sts.
57 Purl one row.
58 k2tog across the row – 3 sts.
Cut yarn leaving a long tail and thread through the remaining three sts.
Press lightly.
Make another the same.

Making up

1 Sew the head with right sides together with a small backstitch.
2 Turn the right side round and attach the eyes.
3 Turn inside out again, and finish sewing up.
4 Stuff lightly.
5 Sew body to tail with an oversew stitch.

Hair

Cut 50cm (20in.) lengths of bouclé yarn and sew in bundles of four strands across the top of the head, back-stitching with the same yarn. Trim as necessary.

Sew on a smile and little eyelashes. Use beads for eyes.

Designed and made by Roz Esposito. Wool by Rowan.

Knitted boyfriend and girlfriend

This inseparable pair are a project for an experienced knitter who has confidence. You can make the dolls look like you and your partner by giving them the right hairstyle and colouring! The ones shown here are wired so they can sit and stand; wire was inserted at the same time as the stuffing, with the stuffing packed around it. They are also wearing simple clothes. To make similar clothes for your dolls you could try adapting one of the patterns at the back of this book.

YOU WILL NEED

- 1 x 250g ball of flesh-coloured double knitting yarn to make both dolls
- Small quantities of coloured yarn for hair and facial detailing

Tension: Should be sufficient so that the stuffing is not visible through completed knit.

Size of each doll: 30cm (12in.) tall

Female Doll Pattern

Left foot

Cast on 12 sts.
st st four rows.
k5, dec1, k5.
Purl one row.

Left heel

k7, sl4.
sl5, p5, sl1.
sl2, k3, sl6.
Purl one row.
sl2, k3, sl6.
sl6, p3, sl2.

Left ankle

k4, dec1, k3, dec1.
Purl one row.

Left lower leg

k4, inc1, k4.
Purl one row.
k4, inc1, k5.
Purl one row.
k5, inc1, k5.
Purl one row.
k5, inc1, k6.
Purl one row.
k6, inc1, k6.

Purl one row.
k6, inc1, k7.
Purl one row.
k7, inc1, k7.
Three rows of st st starting on a purl row.

Left knee
k7, dec1, k7.
p6, dec1, p6, dec1.
k6, dec1, k5.
sl7, p3, sl2.
sl7, k3, sl2.
Purl one row.

Left upper leg
k6, inc1, k5.
Purl one row.
k6, inc1, k6.
Purl one row.
k7, inc1, k6.
Purl one row.
k7, inc1, k7.
Purl one row.
k8, inc1, k7.
Purl one row.
k8, inc1, k8.
Purl one row.
k9, inc1, k8.
Purl one row.
k9, inc1, k9.
Purl one row.
k10, inc1, k9.
Purl one row.
k10, inc1, k9, inc1.
Purl one row.

Slide leg to base of needle and cut yarn, leaving 10–15 cm (4–6 in.) of yarn trailing from final st.

Right foot
Cast on 12 more sts to needle with prior leg attached.
st st 4 rows.
k5, dec1, k5.
Purl one row.

Right heel
sl4, k7.
sl1, p5, sl5.
sl6, k3, sl2.
Purl one row.
sl6, k3, sl2.
sl2, p3, sl6.

Right ankle
dec1, k3, dec1, k4.
Purl one row.

Right lower leg
k4, inc1, k4.
Purl one row.
k5, inc1, k4.
Purl one row.
k5, inc1, k5.
Purl one row.
k6, inc1, k5.
Purl one row.
k6, inc1, k6.
Purl one row.
k7, inc1, k6.
Purl one row.
k7, inc1, k7.
Three rows of st st starting on a purl row.

Right knee
k7, dec1, k7.
dec1, p6, dec1, p6.
k5, dec1, k6.
sl2, p3, sl7.
sl2, k3, sl7.
Purl one row.

Right upper leg
k5, inc1, k6.
Purl one row.
k6, inc1, k6.
Purl one row.
k6, inc1, k7.
Purl one row.
k7, inc1, k7.
Purl one row.
k7, inc1, k8.
Purl one row.
k8, inc1, k8.
Purl one row.
k8, inc1, k9.
Purl one row.
k9, inc1, k9.
Purl one row.
k9, inc1, k10.
Purl one row.

inc1, k9, inc1, k10.
Purl one row.

Both legs should now be on the same needle with the feet pointing in towards the centre (heels pointing outwards).
The first row of the next section of the pattern will involve knitting straight across the top of the two leg pieces, merging them into one piece.

Bottom

inc3, k4, inc1, k30, inc1, k4, inc3.
p11, inc1, p30, inc1, p11.
k16, dec1, k20, dec1, k16.
Purl one row.
k10, dec1, k2, dec1, k22, dec1, k2, dec1, k10.
Purl one row.
dec1, k8, dec1, k26, dec1, k8, dec1.
Purl one row.

Waist

dec1, k5, dec1, k1, dec1, k22, dec1, k1, dec1, k5, dec1.
Purl one row.
dec1, k7, dec1, k18, dec1, k7, dec1.
Purl one row.
k3, dec1, k3, dec1, k16, dec1, k3, dec1, k3.
Purl one row.
k7, dec1, k14, dec1, k7.
Purl one row.
k7, inc1, k14, inc1, k7.
Purl one row.
k8, inc1, k14, inc1, k8.
Purl one row.
k8, inc1, k16, inc1, k8.
Purl one row.
k9, inc1, k16, inc1, k9.
Purl one row.

Chest

k13, inc3, k2, inc2, k2, inc3, k13.
p13, inc1, p8, inc2, p8, inc1, p13.
k14, inc1, k2, inc1, k2, inc1, k2, inc2, k2, inc1, k2, inc1, k2, inc1, k14.
Purl one row.
Knit one row.
p14, dec1, p26, dec1, p14.
k14, dec1, k9, dec1, k2, dec1, k9, dec1, k14.
p14, dec2, p5, dec1, p2, dec1, p5, dec2, p14.
k14, dec1, k3, dec1, k4, dec1, k3, dec1, k14.
Purl one row.

Shoulders

k10, dec1, k18, dec1, k10.
p9, dec1, p18, dec1, p9.
k6, dec3, k14, dec3, k6.
p5, dec3, p10, dec3, p5.
k4, dec3, k6, dec3, k4.
p1, dec4, p2, dec4, p1.

Neck

st st four rows.

Head

inc1, k1, inc1, k2, inc2, k2, inc1, k1, inc1.
p2, inc1, p5, inc2, p5, inc1, p2.
sl10, k2, sl10.
sl9, p4, sl9.
sl10, k2, sl10.
p3, inc1, p5, inc1, p2, inc1, p5, inc1, p3.
k1, inc1, k1, inc1, k6, inc1, k4, inc1, k6, inc1, k1, inc1, k1.
Purl one row.
k10, inc1, k4, inc2, k4, inc1, k10.
sl17, dec1, sl17.
sl17, k1, sl17.
p17, dec1, p16.
st st four rows.
dec 1, k3, dec1, k3, dec1, k10, dec1, k3, dec1, k3, dec1.
p3, dec1, p3, dec1, p8, dec1, p3, dec1, p3.
dec1, k1 repeat to end of row.
p1, dec1 repeat to end of row.
dec to end of row.

Cut yarn and pass through remaining stitches on needle in order to gather together. Tie off, and the main body section is complete.

Right hand

Cast on ten sts.
Knit one row.
Purl one row.
k4, inc1, k5.

st st three rows starting on a purl row.
k4, dec1, k3, dec1.

Right arm

st st three rows starting on a purl row.
k4, inc1, k4.
Complete nine rows of st st.
k2, sl6, k2.
p2, sl6, p2.
k2, sl6, k2.
p9, inc1.
Complete 14 rows of st st.
dec1, k7, dec1.
dec1, p5, dec1.
Knit one row.
dec1, p3, dec1.
dec1, k1, dec1.
Cast off.

Left hand

Cast on ten sts.
st st two rows.
k5, inc1, k4.
st st three rows starting on a purl row.
dec1, k3, dec1, k4.

Left arm

st st three rows starting on a purl row.
k4, inc 1, k4.
Complete nine rows of st st.
k2, sl6, k2.
p2, sl6, p2.
k2, sl6, k2.
inc1, p9.
Complete 14 rows of st st.
dec1, k7, dec1.
dec1, p5, dec1.
Knit one row.
dec1, p3, dec1.
dec1, k1, dec1.
Cast off.

Male Doll Pattern

Left foot

Cast on 12 sts.
st st four rows.
k5, dec1, k5.
Purl one row.

Left heel

k7, sl4.
sl5, p5, sl1.
sl2, k3, sl6.
Purl one row.
sl2, k3, sl6.
sl6, p3, sl2.

Left ankle

k4, dec1, k3, dec1.
Purl one row.

Left lower leg

k4, inc1, k4.
Purl one row.
Knit one row.
p4, inc1, p5.
Knit one row.
Purl one row.
k5, inc1, k5.
Purl one row.
Knit one row.
p5, inc1, p6.
Knit one row.
Purl one row.
k6, inc1, k6.
st st 3 rows starting on a purl row.

Left knee

k6, dec1, k6.
p2, dec1, p9.
Knit one row.
sl2, k3, sl7.
Purl one row.

Left upper leg

k6, inc1, k5.
Purl one row.
Knit one row.
p6, inc1, p6.
Knit one row.
Purl one row.
k7, inc1, k6.
Purl one row.
Knit one row.
p7, inc1, p7.
Knit one row.
Purl one row.
k8, inc1, k7.
Purl one row.
Knit one row.
p8, inc1, p8.
Knit one row.
Purl one row.

k9, inc1, k8.
Purl one row.

Slide leg to base of needle and cut yarn, leaving 10–15cm (4–6in.) of yarn trailing from final stitch.

Right foot

Cast on 12 sts (to needle with prior leg attached).
st st 4 rows.
k5, dec1, k5.
Purl one row.

Right heel

sl4, k7.
sl1, p5, sl5.
sl6, k3, sl2.
Purl one row.
sl6, k3, sl2.
sl2, p3, sl6.

Right ankle

dec1, k3, dec1, k4.
Purl one row.

Right lower leg

k4, inc1, k4.
Purl one row.
Knit one row.
p5, inc1, p4.
Knit one row.
Purl one row.
k5, inc1, k5.
Purl one row.
Knit one row.
p6, inc 1, p5.
Knit one row.
Purl one row.
k6, inc1, k6.
st st 3 rows starting on a purl row.

Right knee

k6, dec1, k6.
p9, dec1, p2.
Knit one row.
sl2, p3, sl7.
sl7, k3, sl2.
Purl one row.

Right upper leg

k5, inc1, k6.
Purl one row.
Knit one row.
p6, inc1, p6.
Knit one row.
Purl one row.
k6, inc1, k7.
Purl one row.
Knit one row.
p7, inc1, p7.
Knit one row.
Purl one row.
k7, inc1, k8.
Purl one row.
Knit one row.
p8, inc1, p8.
Knit one row.
Purl one row.
k8, inc1, k9.
Purl one row.

Both legs should now be on the same needle with the feet pointing in towards the centre (i.e. heels pointing outwards).
The first row of the next section of the pattern will involve knitting straight across the top of the two leg pieces, merging them into one piece.

Bottom

inc2, k3, inc1, k26, inc1, k3, inc2.
p8, inc1, p26, inc1, p8.
Knit one row.
Purl one row.
k7, dec1, k28, dec1, k7.
Purl one row.

Waist

dec1, k5, dec1, k26, dec1, k5, dec1.
Purl one row.
k9, dec1, k18, dec1, k9.
st st three rows starting on a purl row.

Chest

k9, inc1, k18, inc1, k9.
Purl one row.
Knit one row.
p10, inc1, p18, inc1, p10.
Knit one row.
Purl one row.
k10, inc1, k20, inc1, k10.
Purl one row.
Knit one row.

p11, inc1, p20, inc1, p11.
Knit one row.
Purl one row.
k11, inc1, k3, inc1, k5, inc1, k2, inc1, k5, inc1, k3, inc1, k11.
st st 7 rows.
k10, dec1, k3, dec1, k18, dec1, k3, dec1, k10.
Purl one row.

Shoulders

k9, dec3, k18, dec3, k9.
p8, dec3, p14, dec3, p8.
k6, dec3, k12, dec3, k6.
p4, dec3, p10, dec3, p4.
k3, dec3, k6, dec3, k3.
p4, dec2, p2, dec2, p4

Neck

st st 4 rows.

Head

k1, inc1, k4, inc2, k4, inc1, k1.
p2, inc1, p4, inc1, p2, inc1, p4, inc1, p2.
sl10, k2, sl10.
sl9, p4, sl9.
sl10, k2, sl10.
p3, inc1, p5, inc1, p2, inc1, p5, inc1, p3.
k1, inc1, k1, inc1, k18, inc1, k1, inc1, k1.
Purl one row.
k9, inc1, k4, inc2, k4, inc1, k9.
sl16, p2, sl16.
sl16, k2, sl16.
Purl one row.
k16, dec1, p16.
st st 3 rows starting on a purl row.
dec1, k3, dec1, k18, dec1, k3, dec1.
p2, dec1, p3, dec1, p9, dec1, p3, dec1, p2.
k3, dec1, k3, dec1, k9, dec1, k3, dec1, k3.
dec1, p1 repeat to end of row.
k1, dec1 repeat to end of row.
dec to end of row.

Cut yarn and pass through remaining on needle in order to gather together. Tie off, and the main body section is complete.

Right hand

Cast on 11 sts.
st st 2 rows.
k5, inc 1, k5.
st st 3 rows starting on a purl row.
k4, dec1, k4, dec1.

Right arm

st st 3 rows starting on a purl row.
k4, inc1, k5.
st st 10 rows.
p2, sl6, p3.
k3, sl6, k2.
p2, sl6, p3.
k10, inc1.
Purl one row.
k4, inc1, k7.
st st 5 rows.
k4, dec1, k7.
p6, inc1, p5.
st st 7 rows.
dec1, p9, dec1.
dec1, k7, dec1.
dec1, p5, dec1.
Knit one row.
dec1, p3, dec1.
dec1, k1, dec1.
Cast off.

Left hand

Cast on 11 sts.
st st 2 rows.
k5, inc1, k5.
st st 3 rows starting on a purl row.
dec1, k4, dec1, k4.

Left arm

st st 3 rows starting on a purl row.
k5, inc1, k4.
st st 10 rows.
p3, sl6, p2.
k2, sl6, k3.
p3, sl6, p2.
inc1, k10.
Purl one row.
k7, inc1, k4.
st st 5 rows.
k7, dec1, k4.
p5, inc1, p6.
st st 7 rows.
dec1, p9, dec1.
dec1, k7, dec1.

dec1, p5, dec1.
Knit one row.
dec1, p3, dec1.
dec1, k1, dec1.
Cast off.

Making up

1 Stitch up the leg using the same coloured yarn, inserting small quantities of stuffing as you go in order to achieve good shape. If the doll is to be wired, take a piece of wire a little longer than the length of the doll's body and form a small loop at one end to sit in the foot. This will prevent the wire from poking out of the foot. When the wire is in place, pack the stuffing around it and stitch the leg up.
2 Repeat for other leg.
3 Stitch up the back of the doll, again, stuffing as you go. If the doll is to be wired, take the two wires emerging from the upper legs and twist together to form a 'backbone'. Insert the stuffing around the wire and sew the doll closed.
4 Stitch the back of the head to close. If the doll is to be wired, form the top of the wire emerging from the torso into a loop, to prevent the end of the wire emerging from the head. Stuff around the wire and sew closed as before.
5 Stitch arms closed, stuffing throughout. If the doll is to be wired, take a second piece of wire about three times the length of one arm, and feed through one of the arms and into the torso at the shoulder. Form a loop at the end to sit in the hand, stuff and stitch the arm closed. Stitch the arm to the upper body.
6 Stitch the other arm closed around the wire protruding from other shoulder, stuffing throughout. Attach the arm to the shoulder.
7 Sew on the facial features and the hair. I have used knitting yarn for all the facial detail, but embroidery threads could also be used.

Designed and made by Charlotte Ladner.

Boyfriend and girlfriend became Mr and Mrs...

4. Rag dolls

Traditional rag doll

This doll with removable clothes, wool hair and a hand-embroidered face is the type you might make for a child. Alternatively, try personalising it with a certain type of clothing or with distinguishing features like a certain style or colour of hair, freckles or glasses, to make a 'mini me'. It is designed for a more experienced maker.

YOU WILL NEED

- 2 head pieces (see p.141)
- 4 arm pieces
- 4 leg pieces
- 2 body pieces
- Fabric for clothes
- Wool for hair
- Embroidery thread for face

Place pattern pieces on fabric and cut out with care.

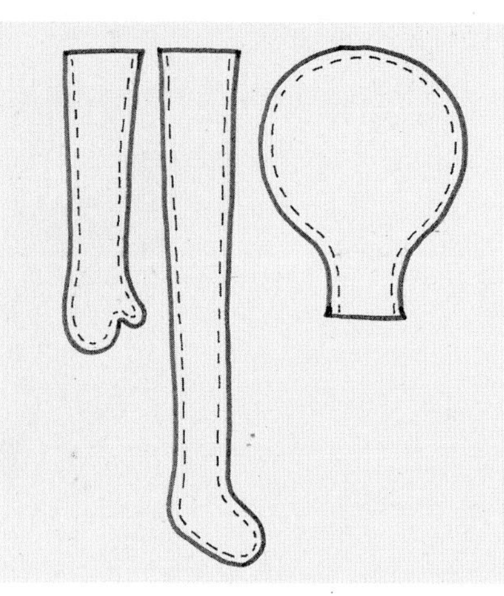

1 With the right sides together, stitch the arm, leg and head pieces leaving one end open as shown.

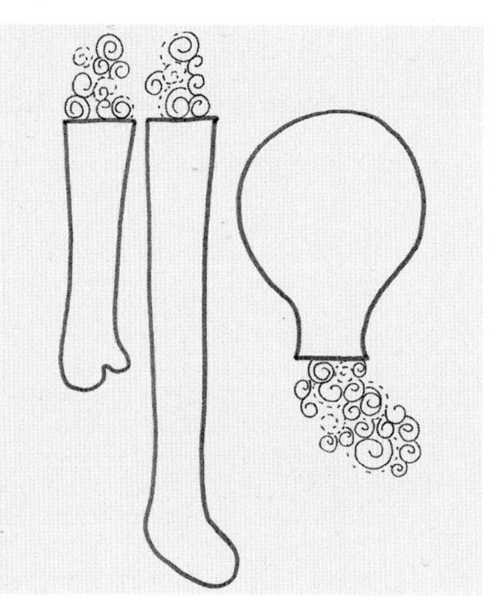

2 Turn to the right side and stuff all three pieces. Stuff the head and neck firmly, making sure the neck is stiff.

3 With the right sides together, stitch the front and back of the body together at the shoulders and side seams.

4 Turn to the right side.

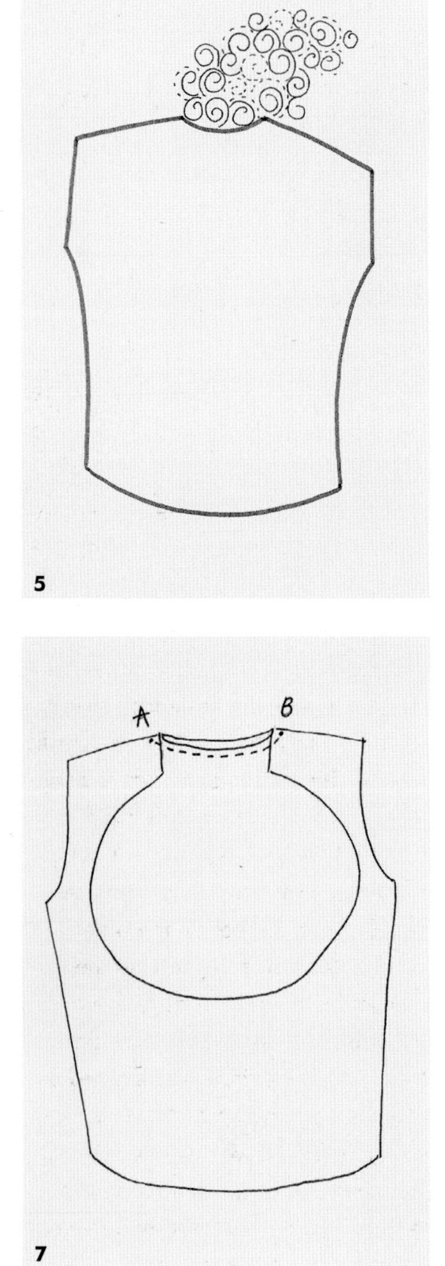

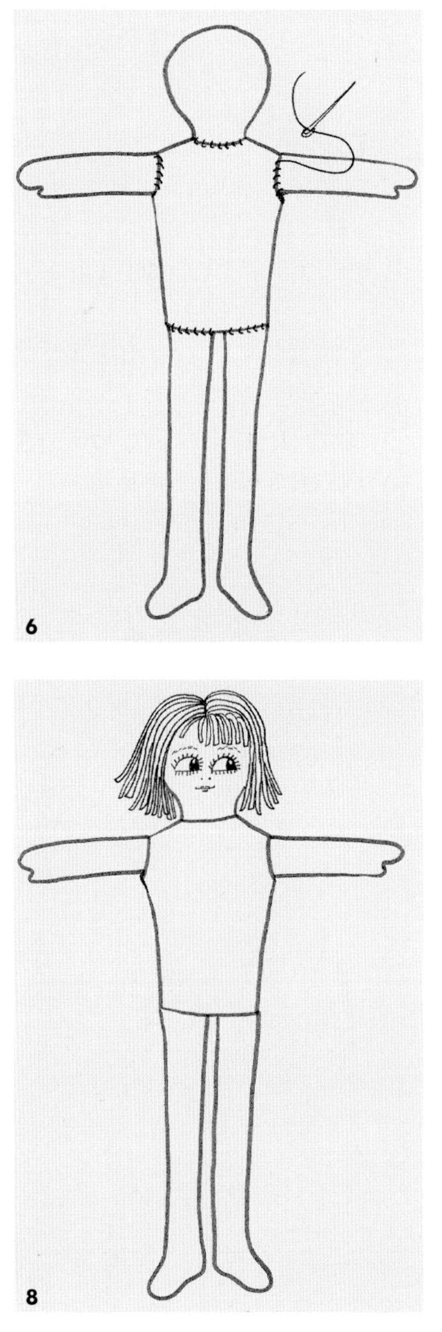

5 Insert the head into the neck opening, and pull the unstuffed body over the head, as shown. Attach the inside of the neck seam to the stuffed neck by hand, using tiny stitches. Pull the body down into position. The stitches will be on the inside of the body. Do the same with both arms. With the head and arms in place, stuff the body.

6 Prepare the legs initially by matching the seams at the top, then by displacing them 0.5cm (¼in.) off centre to allow the legs to 'kick out'. Poke the legs into the body and tack in position, before oversewing the legs to the body to attach them.

7 This shows the wrong side of the fabric. The right sides are touching, and the head is inside the body.

8 Add wool hair by couching down strands across the back of the head and stitching down in the 'parting' line from the top to the bottom of the head. The face on this doll is hand-embroidered using a satin stitch for the eyes and the mouth.

Designed and made by Laura Hoile.

Mouse in a knitted dress

This creature has a face made of three panels but is essentially is based on a traditional rag doll. The mouse here is made from linen but you could choose any fabric, patterned or plain, and the dress is simply a tube of plain knitting shaped at the neck. I made a hat by gluing a cylinder of card covered with fabric to a fabric-covered circular base – just to give the mouse a debonair look. Stitches on the feet and hands make them into paws!

YOU WILL NEED

- 1 face piece (see p.140)
- 2 face side pieces
- 2 body pieces
- 4 arm pieces
- 4 leg pieces
- 2 tail pieces
- 4 ear pieces
- Thread to stitch face and other details

Place the pattern pieces onto fabric and cut out with care.

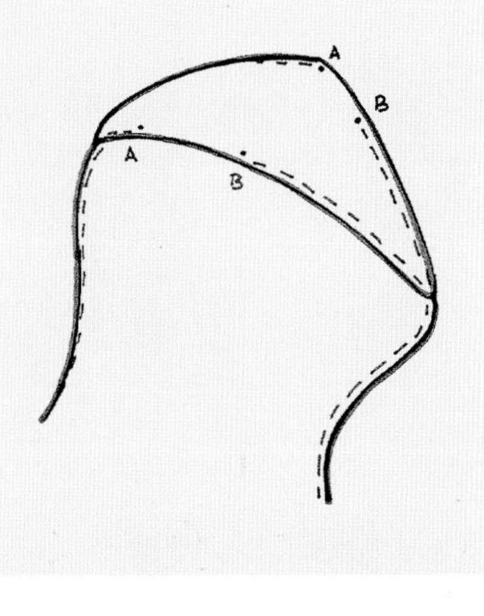

1 Pin and tack the three face pieces, right sides together, so that they make a head shape as shown. Start sewing on one side at the point marked A and continue to the point at the nape of the neck where the top and side panels meet. Repeat on the other side and continue the sewing line, joining the two side panels together to the bottom edge of the side panel. Next start at the first point marked B, continuing to the tip of the nose. The second row from the point marked B must continue through the nose tip to the edge of the side panel, joining two the side panels together.

2

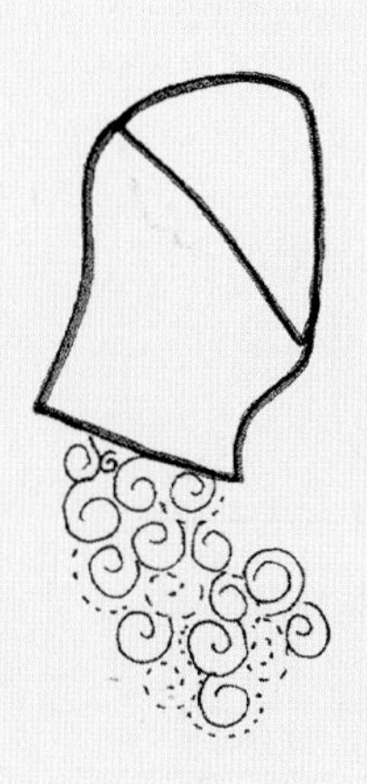

3

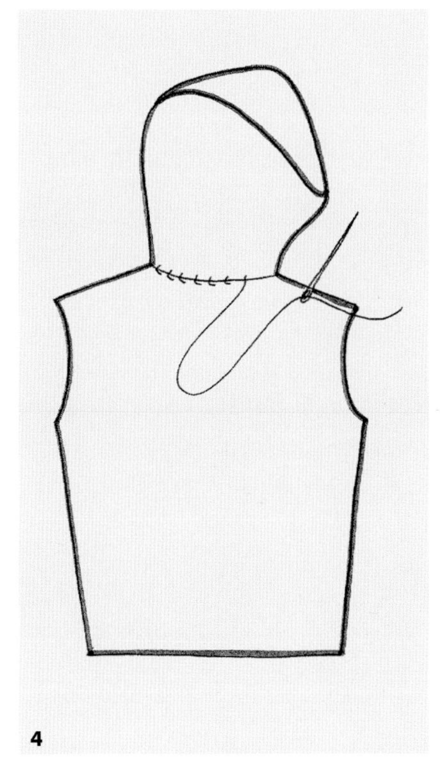

4

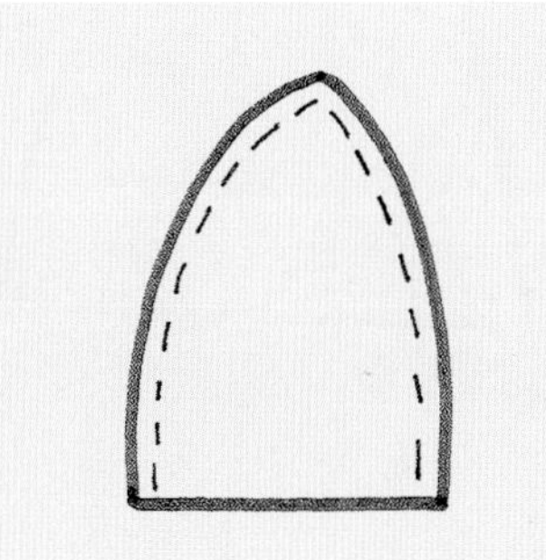

5

6

2 With the right sides together, stitch the shoulder and side seams.

3 Turn to the right side and stuff the body and head.

4 Poke the head into the body and pin and tack through the layers – front, stuffing, back – to hold it in position before oversewing the neck to the body.

5 With right sides together, stitch the ear pieces together. Repeat for the second ear.

6 Turn the ears to the right side and make a running stitch along the bottom edge of the ear. Gather the fabric along the running stitch to shape the ear.

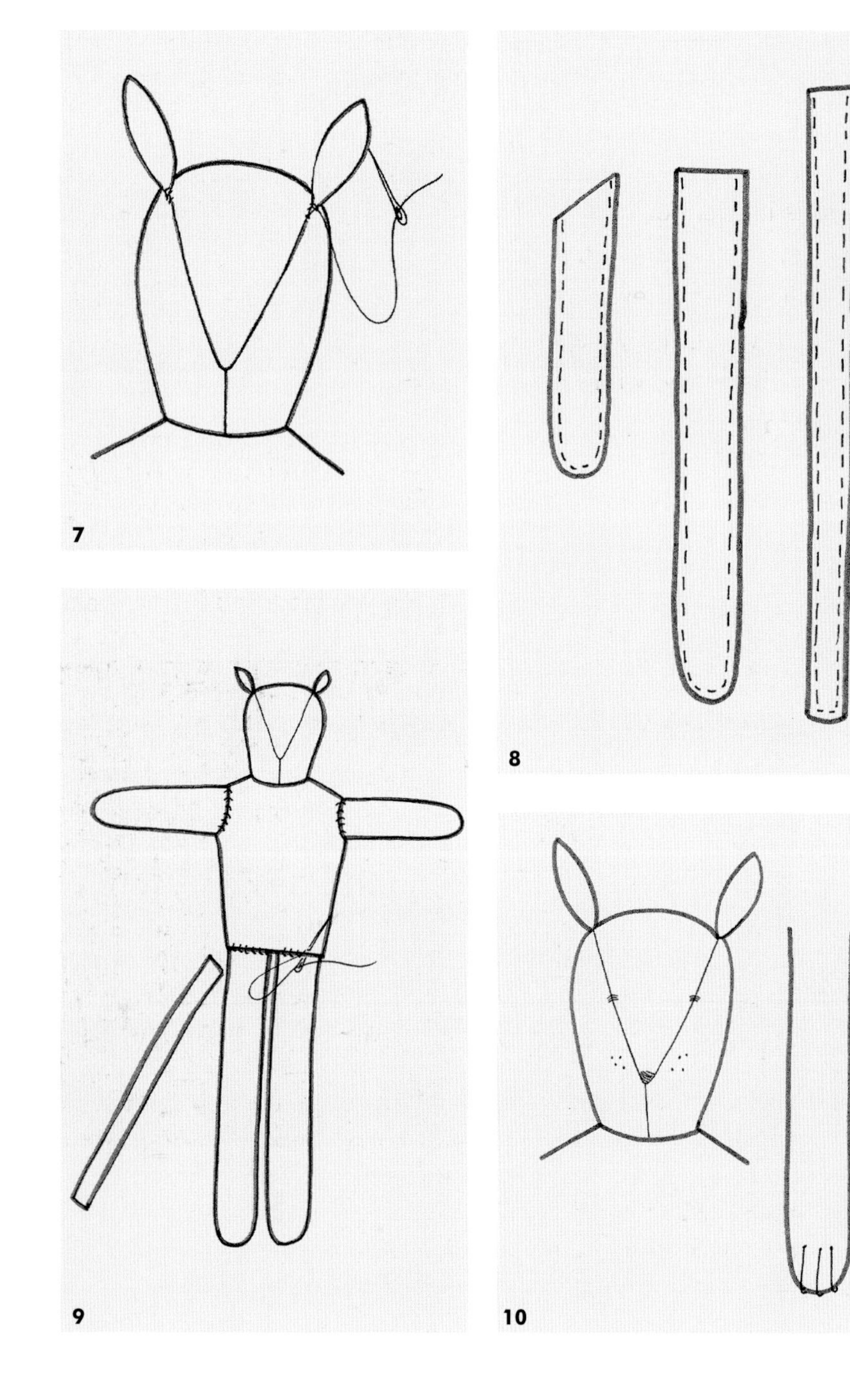

7 Poke the ears into gaps left at the top of the head (A to B) and stitch into position.

8 With the right sides together stitch the limb pieces together, leaving the top edge open as shown, creating two arms, two legs and a tail. Turn to the right side and stuff the limbs. You can also stuff the tail if you want it to be fat, though I left mine unstuffed and skinny.

9 Poke the limbs inside the body in the same way as the head, tacking into position by pushing the needle through the layers – front, stuffing, back – before oversewing the arms, then the legs, to the body. The tail is attached by a few tiny stitches.

10 The face and some markings on the paws and tail can be made by using decorative stitches with thread of normal thickness (i.e. not embroidery thread).

Dress designed and knitted by Mandie Misell.

Long-legged doll

This rag doll is designed so that her dress is in fact her body, while her legs are made of patterned fabric, as if she is wearing tights. The clothes she wears are not detachable, as they are part of her! The long-legged doll is an easier make than the traditional doll, and can be made to look quite funky, with hair which is also a printed fabric, and a quirky face.

YOU WILL NEED

- 2 head pieces (see p.136)
- 2 dress pieces
- 4 arm pieces
- 4 leg pieces
- 2 hair pieces
- Ribbons to tie the hair, buttons for the eyes, and embroidery thread for the cheeks and lips
- Trim for the neck and hem of the skirt

Place the pattern pieces on the fabric and cut out with care.

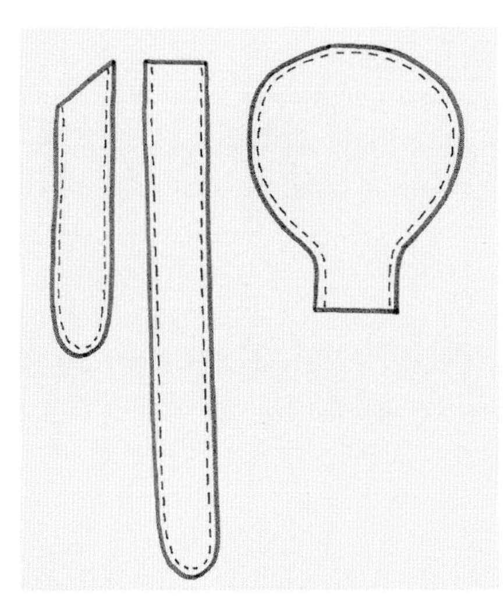

1 With the right sides together, sew the arm, leg and head pieces together, leaving the top of the limbs and the base of the neck open.

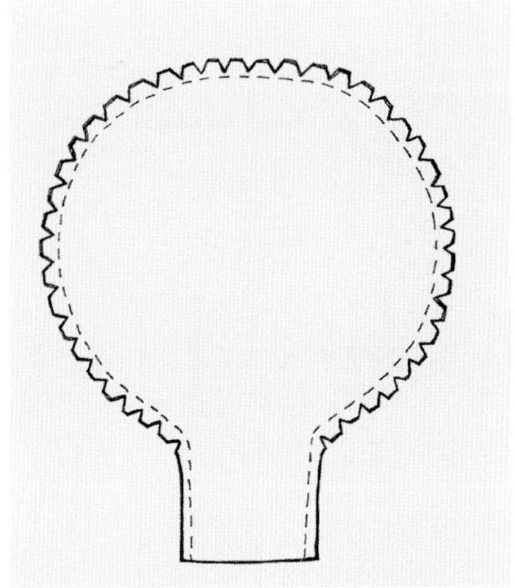

2 Clip the seam allowances of the head piece so that the curves are eased.

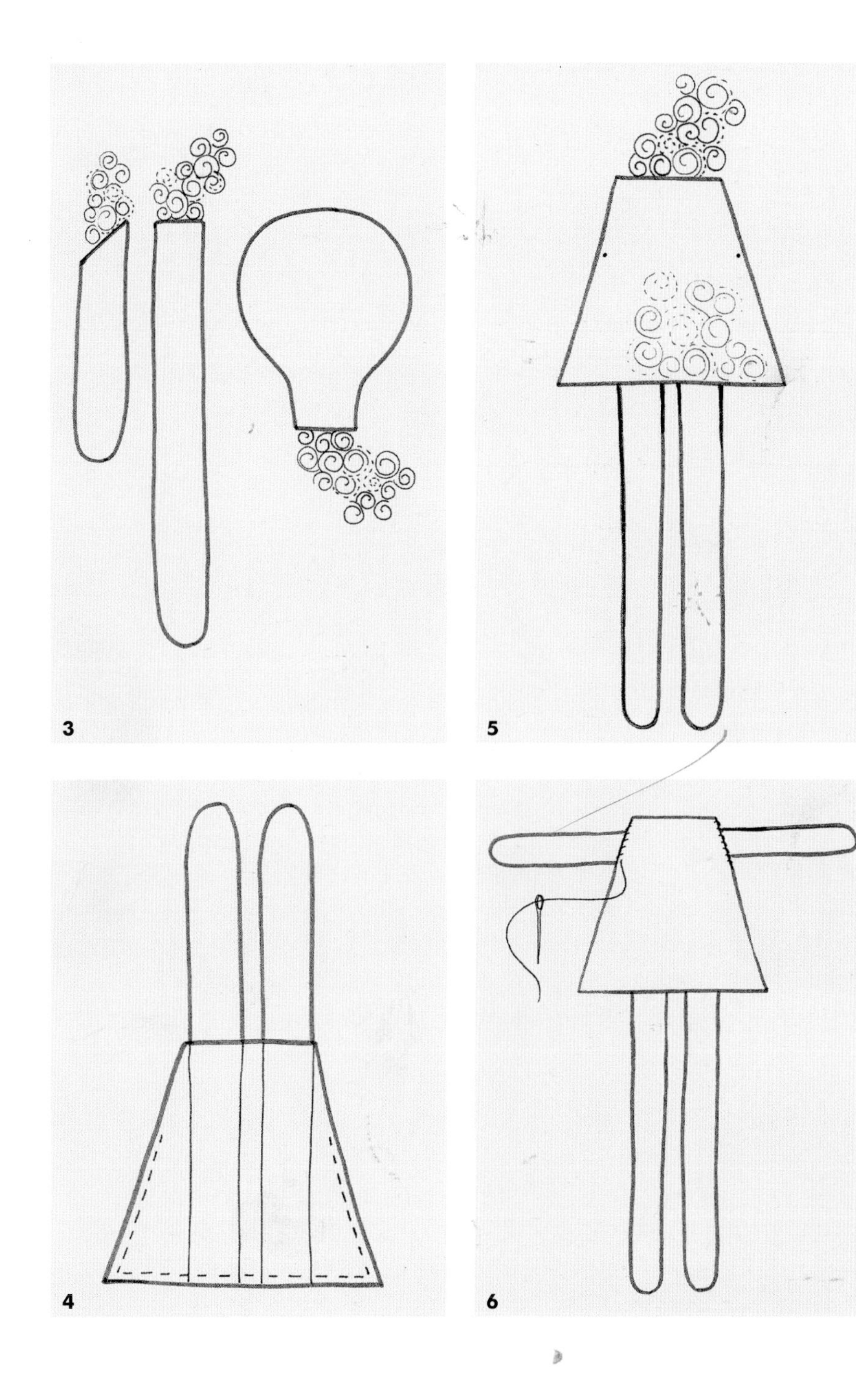

3 Turn to the right side and stuff all the pieces, making sure the head piece is firmly stuffed whilst leaving the limb pieces less firmly stuffed at the top. Pin across the top of the limbs and the base of the neck to keep the stuffing in place.

4 Place the first dress piece onto a surface with the right side of the fabric facing up. Place the newly formed legs on top of the dress piece. Place the second dress piece on top of the legs and also on top of the first dress piece. This will form a 'leg sandwich', and the wrong side of the top dress piece will be facing you. The two dress pieces will now be right sides together. Pin and then tack through the legs to hold them in place, before stitching, using the sewing machine for durability (if you have one), along the bottom edge and halfway up each side seam.

5 Turn to the right side so that the legs now dangle downwards. Stuff the dress up to the dots.

6 Place the arm pieces in position. Pin and tack before sewing through the three layers (dress piece, arm, and top dress layer). This is best done by hand with small stitches.

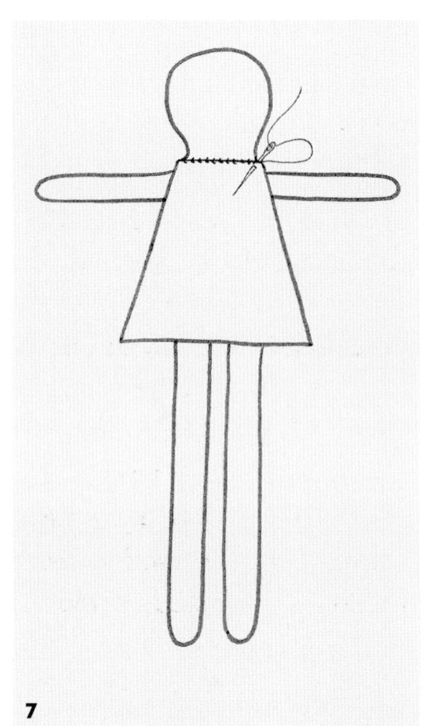

7

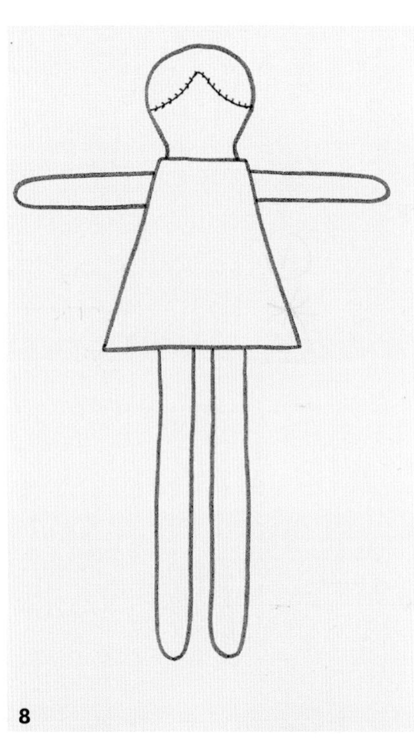

8

9

10

7 Stuff the remainder of the dress, and tack along the top edge of the neck to stop the stuffing coming out. Next, poke the head piece through the tacking stitches into the neck opening, and tack through the three layers (dress, head, and top dress layer) before securing the neck and head in place using tiny hand stitches.

8 Place the fabric 'wig' on the head and sew to the head using tiny stitches.

9 Add on bunches which are shaped by tying with ribbon, as well as buttons for eyes and star-stitched rosy cheeks. The mouth is a French knot. Add on the pom-pom trim at the hem and neckline of dress.

10 If you would like to have a little bird sit on the hand of your long-legged doll, make this by placing two bird pieces with the wrong sides together, and oversewing around the edge of the bird. Leave a 2cm (¾in.) gap at the tummy. Stuff the bird, before oversewing the gap to close it. I embellished the bird with sequins and gave him a bead for an eye.

Try a different-shaped 'wig' of hair and hand-stitched sleepy eyes (see pp.130–1 for inspiration).

Fox puppet

Mr Fox is a quick and relatively easy make using a sewing machine. A rag doll with seamed limbs for extra movement, he can also have strings to make him into a working puppet. Using synthetic fur means that any mistakes or big stitches are not visible as the pile covers small blemishes. Use a wider seam allowance, though – say, 2.5cm (1in.) – if you decide to use fur. The waistcoat should ideally be tweed or wool.

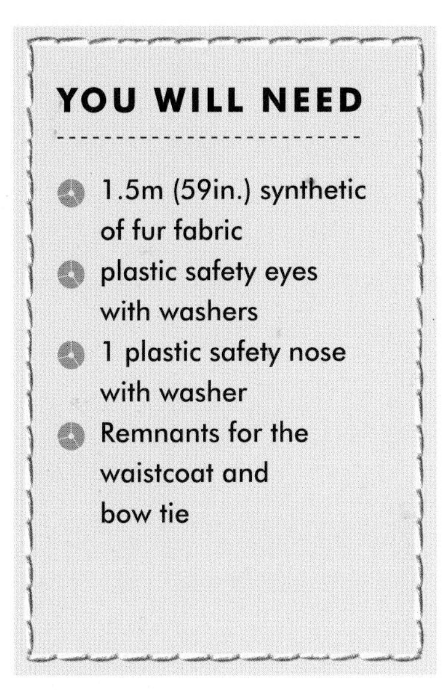

YOU WILL NEED

- 1.5m (59in.) synthetic of fur fabric
- plastic safety eyes with washers
- 1 plastic safety nose with washer
- Remnants for the waistcoat and bow tie

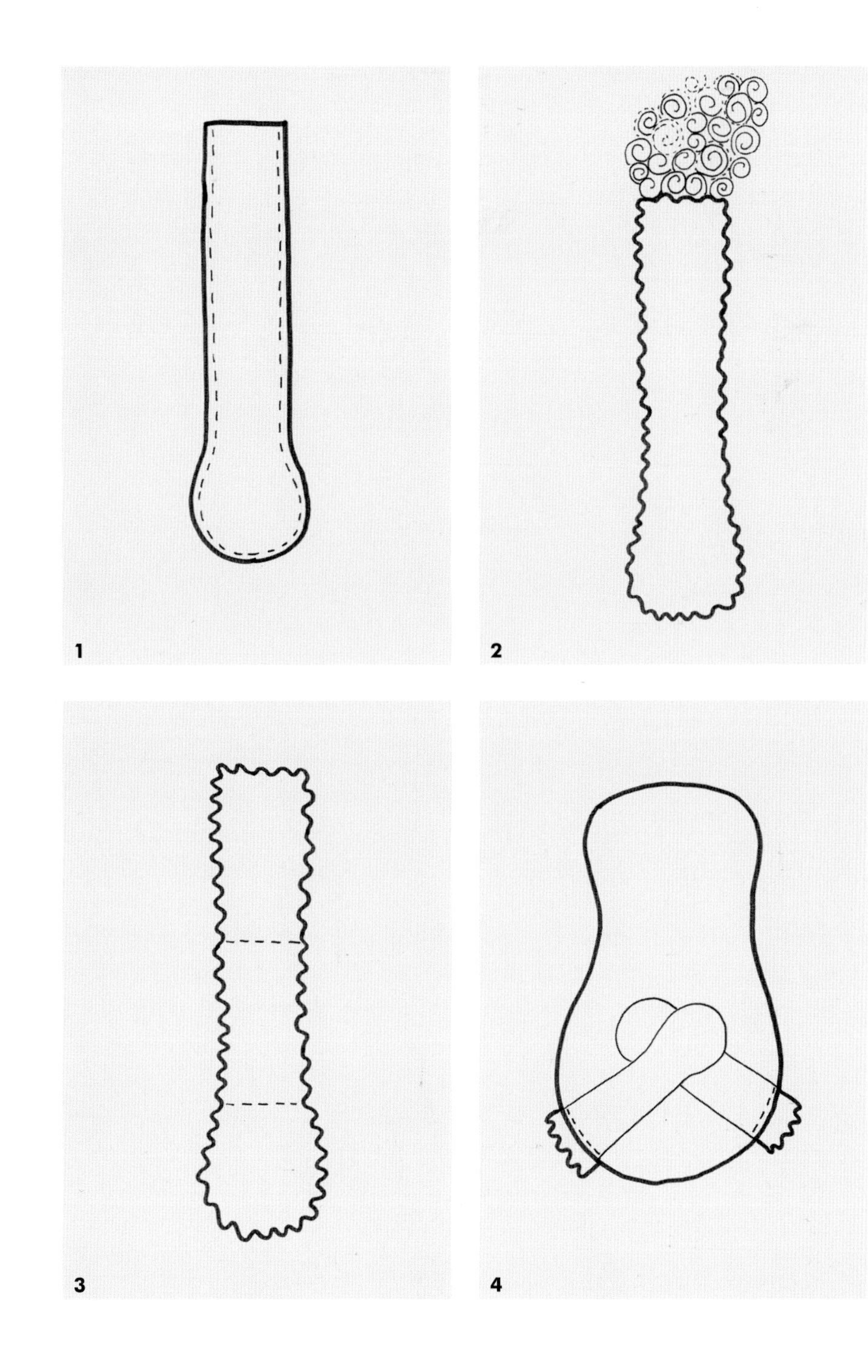

Place the pattern pieces on fabric and cut out with care.

1 With right sides together, pin, tack and sew three sides of the legs leaving the top open to stuff. Repeat this process to make the arms.

2 Stuff the foot of each leg and halfway up the leg.

3 Create a seam by sewing a row of stitches across the right side of the leg in order to create a joint.

Next, stuff the upper leg to the top. Repeat this technique with the arms. Stuff the hand and lower arm before creating an elbow joint by sewing across the arm.

4 With right sides together, pin the front and back body pieces together. Arrange the legs in position by putting them inside the body, making the top of the leg poke 2cm (¾in.) out of the edge of the body. Pin and tack to hold in position.

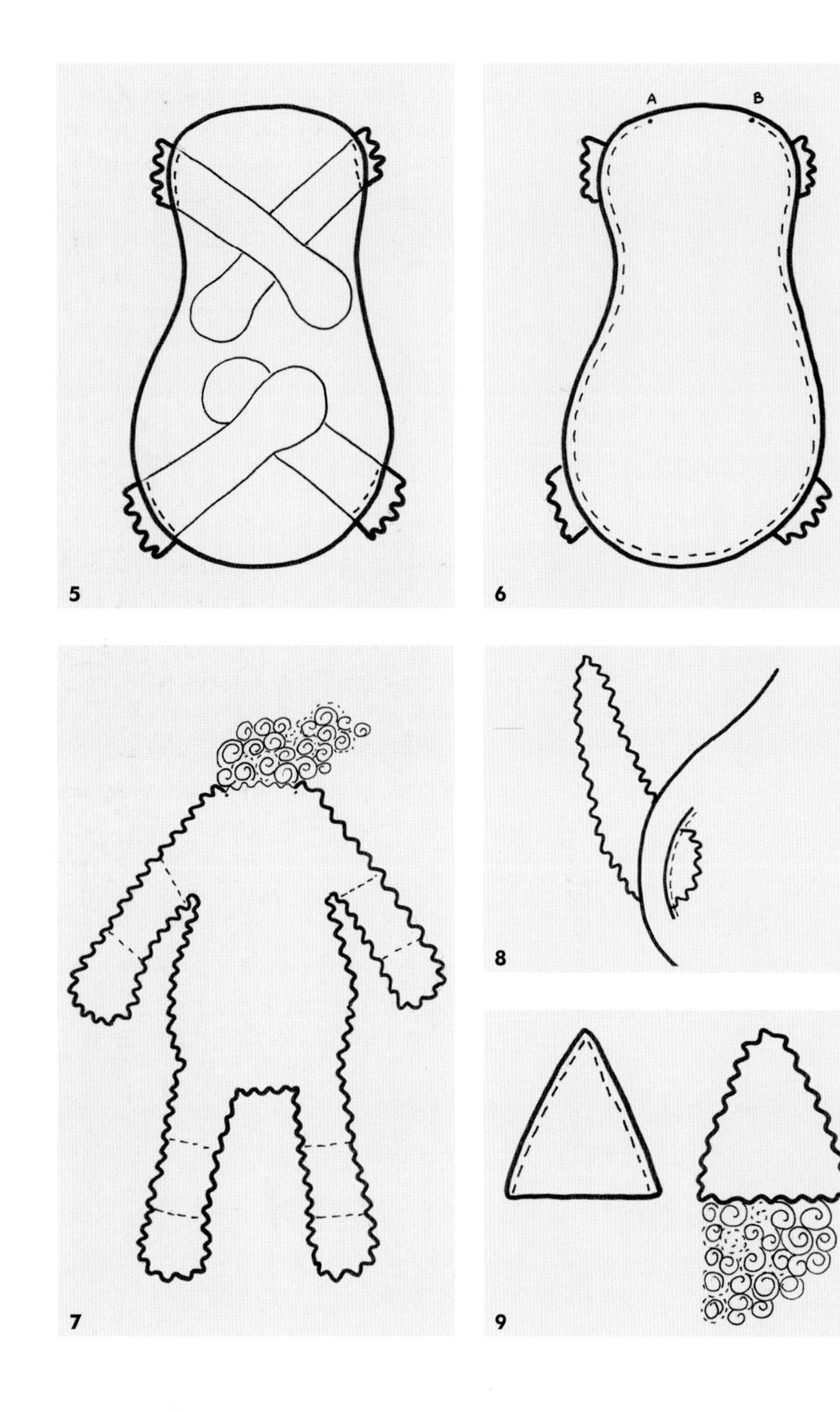

5 Place the arms inside the body, angling them into the position in which they'll be sewn, and making the top of the arm poke 2cm (¾in.) out of the edge of the body. Pin and tack in position.

6 Sew around the body shape from A to B leaving a 6cm (2⅜in.) opening. Be careful that you sew through all layers to ensure that the arms and legs are fixed in position by the stitching.

7 Turn the fox right side out and the limbs will now be in place. Stuff the body, making the tummy nice and stout.

8 Attach the tail by making a small slit in the back of the body and poking the tail in. Pinch the slit fabric into a dart and sew the tail inside the dart so that the stitches are not visible from the outside.

9 With right sides together, pin, tack and sew the ear pieces together. Turn to the right side and stuff.

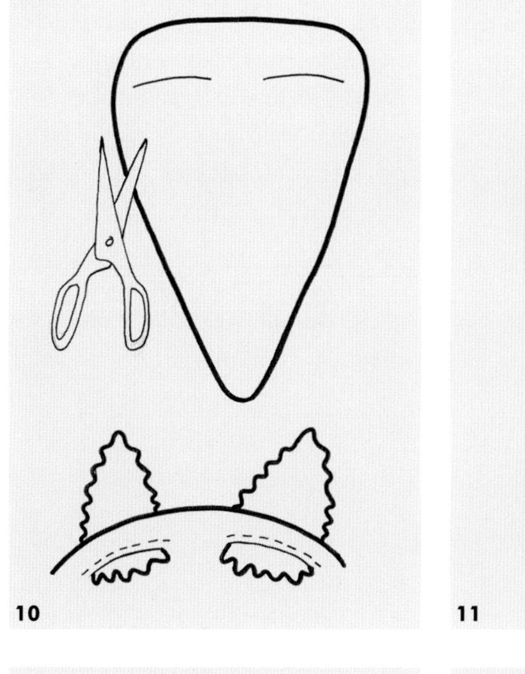

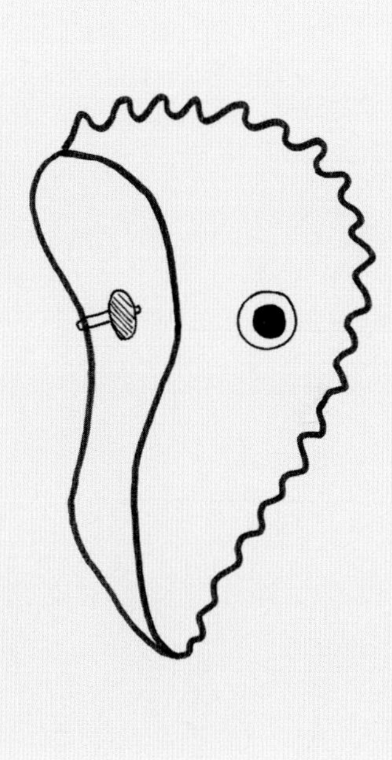

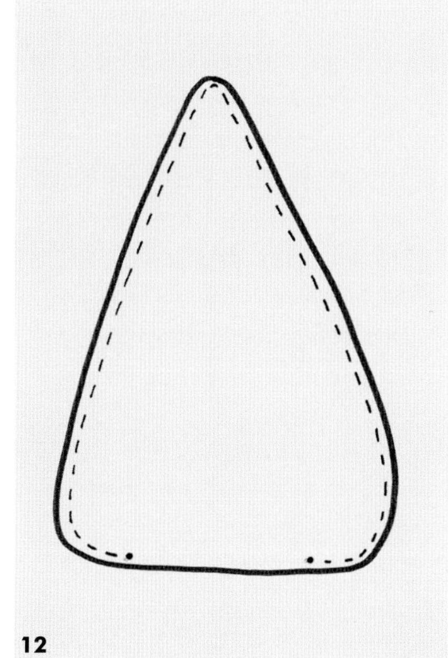

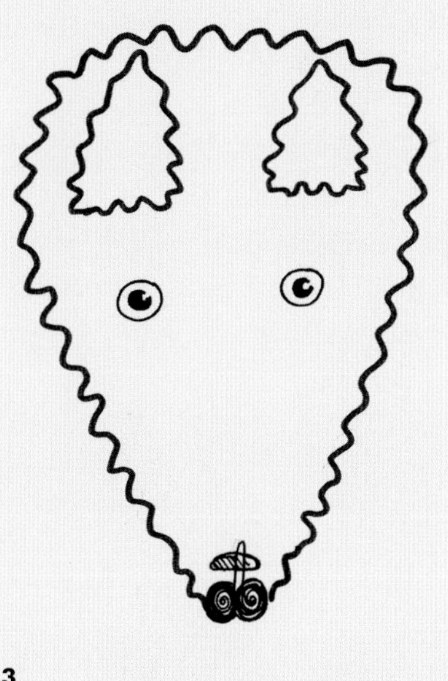

10 Make two slits on the top of the first head piece and poke the ears in. Sew in place by pinching fabric right side to right side to create a dart on the wrong side of the head. The ears will be sewn inside the dart so that the stitches are not visible from the outside.

11 Insert the eyes through the top of the right side of the head and secure with washers.

12 With right sides together, place the second head piece on top of the first and sew two edges leaving the shortest edge open as shown.

13 Turn the head to the right side. Insert the nose into the front seam and secure with a washer.

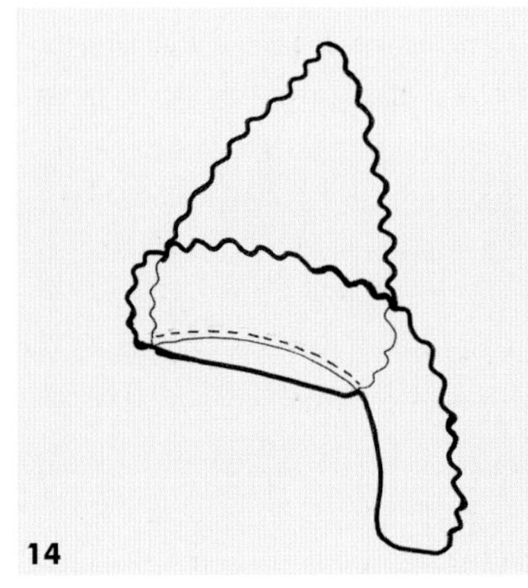
14

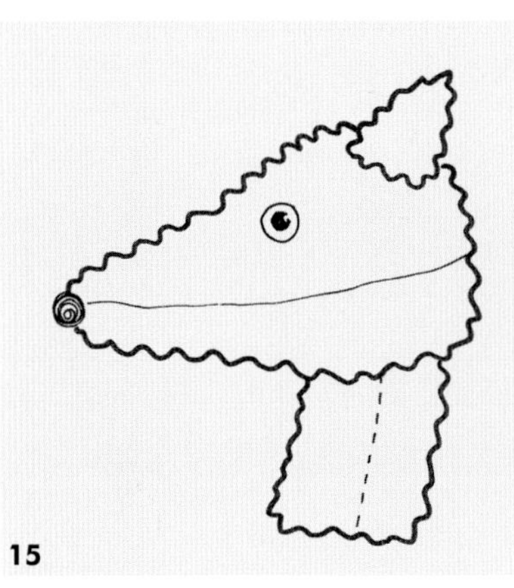
15

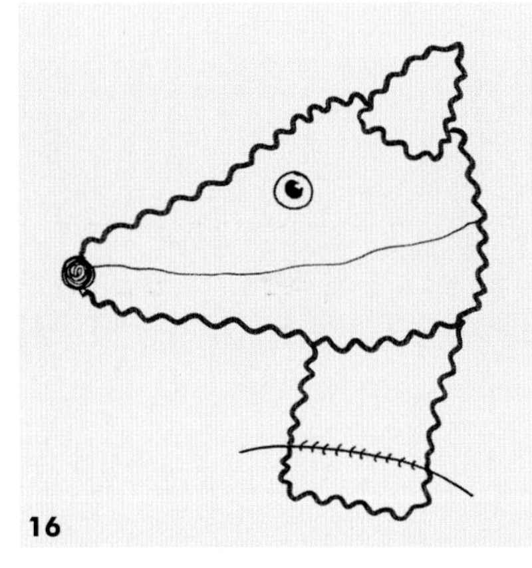
16

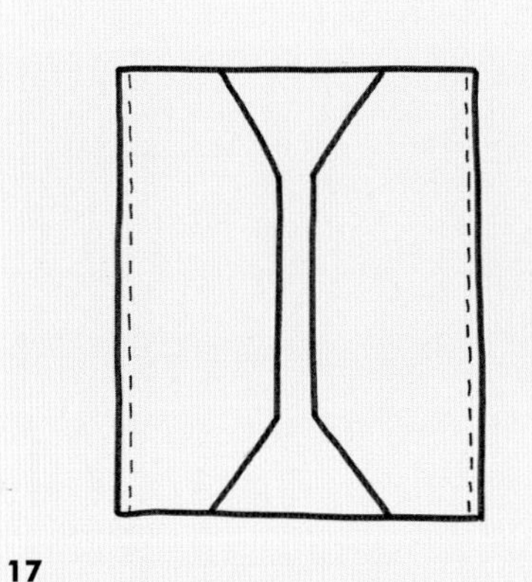
17

18

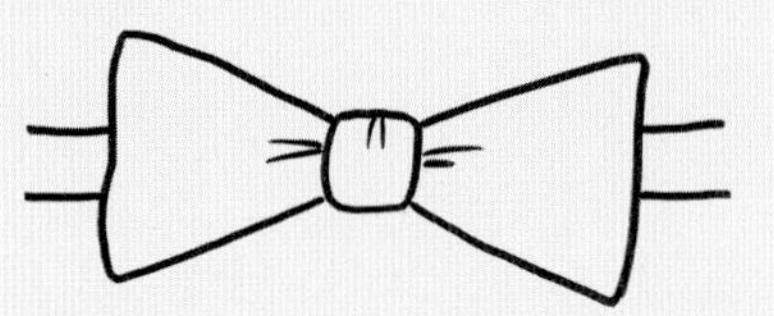
19

14 Stuff the head. Using the pattern piece for the neck, sew the top edge around the edges of the head opening. Manipulate the top of the neck piece to fit around the opening of the head, then stitch.

15 With the neck secured around the base of the head, sew up the side seam of the neck piece.

16 Stuff the neck and poke the bottom of the neck into the hole left at the top of the body. Secure the head into the body using a hand stitch.

17 With the right sides facing eachother, sew the waistcoat pieces together as indicated. Hold the waistcoat against your fox and judge the size of armhole required to fit the circumference of his arms. Mark the position of the armholes on the waistcoat as a semicircle on each side. Cut this out, then hem the raw edges by turning under to create a neat seam.

18 For the bow tie, sew two pieces with the right sides together as indicated, leaving a 3cm (1¼in.) gap.

19 Turn to the right side and tie a separate fabric piece around the

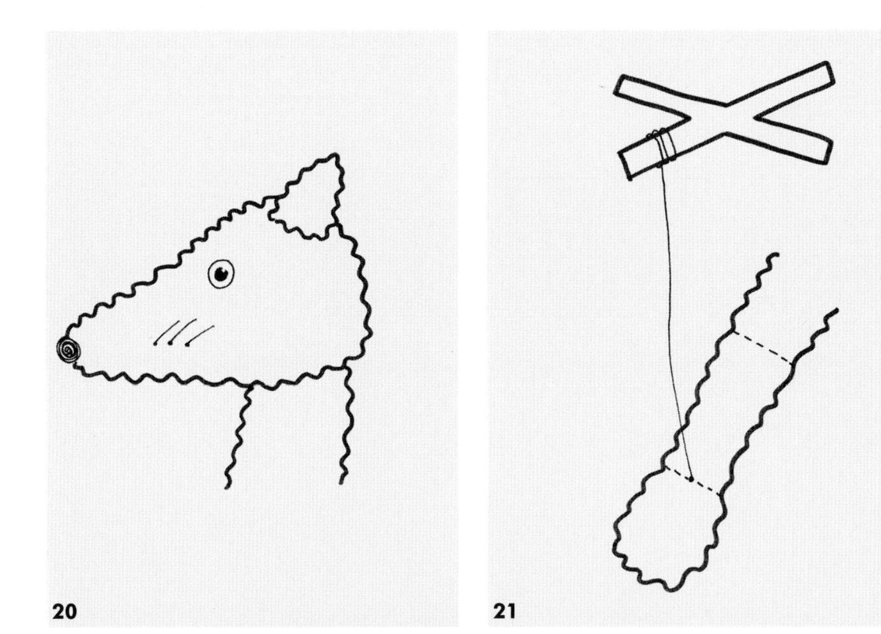

centre to create a bow. Attach this to the neck of the fox with hand stitches.

20 Add detail such as eyebrows or whiskers to the foxy face and flecks of colour to the tail by looping and sewing lengths of wool onto the surface of the fabric.

21 Add strings by sewing in place a length of string to the feet, knees, elbows, hands and head. Tie the top end of the string to a wooden cross.

Fox puppet designed and made by Emily Durham.

5. One-hour makes

Pipe cleaner doll

This doll takes only sixty minutes to make and his small size (six inches tall) means he is easy to manage. He is made from pipe cleaners and fabric remnants. You can use any material you like for his clothes – here he is dressed in colourful, shiny fabrics and metallic threads because they seemed to suit him.

YOU WILL NEED

- 3 extra-long or 5 standard pipe cleaners, twisted together to make a 76cm (30in.) length of wire (alternatively use a 76cm/30in. length of wire)
- One leg of a pair of old tights
- Fabric remnants
- Beads and sequins

1 Place the pattern pieces for the clothes (see p.135) on the fabric and cut out with care.

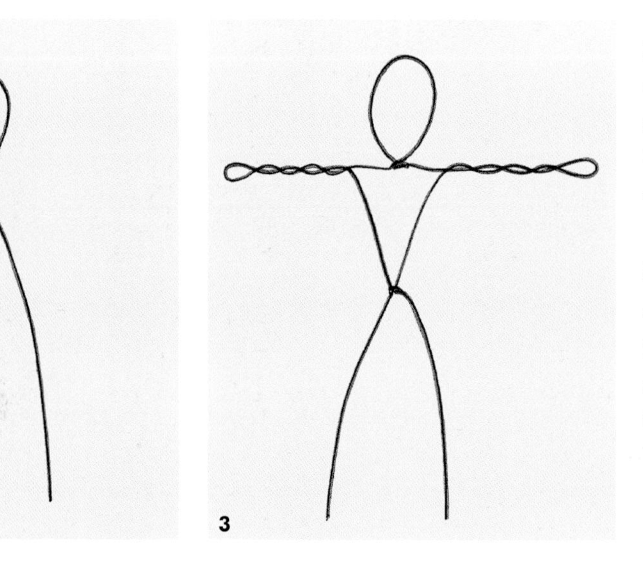

2 Fold the wire in half to make an upside-down 'V' shape. Create a loop in the middle as follows: insert one finger in the fold and twist to make the loop.

3 Bend back each end of wire about 5cm (2in.) from the twist, and then twist to make an arm on each side, leaving a loop at each end for the hands.

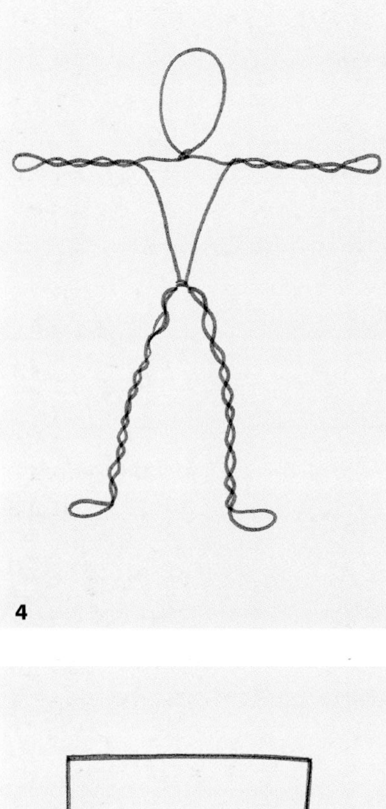

4

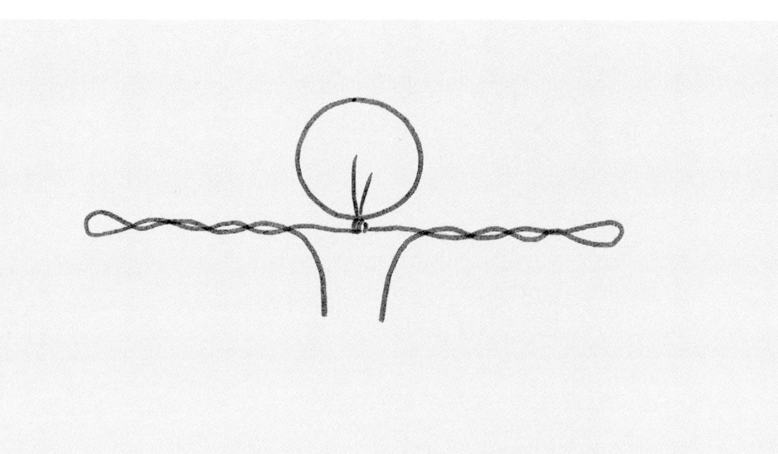

5

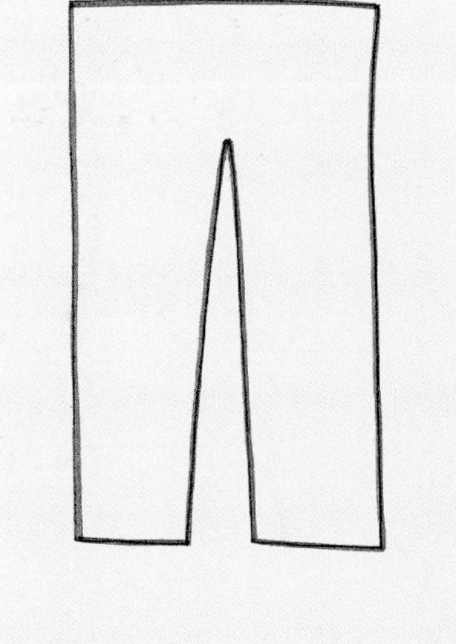

7

4 Bring the ends of the wire together and twist together at the 'waist' to form a triangular body.

Bend back the remaining ends of wire and twist around the waist forming two loops of wire, which will become the legs. Twist the wire, leaving two loops for the feet.

5 Create a round, padded head by stuffing the foot end of the leg of the tights. To do this, cut several strips from the leg of the tights and pack them snugly into the foot of the tights to give it shape. Cut the loop at the top end of the doll, to create two straight pieces of wire. Poke these in to the newly-formed head.

6 Wrap a long strip of tights fabric around the arms, legs and body part of the doll. Secure the end of the fabric in place with tiny stitches and fix the head to the body with a slip stitch. Pad the hands and feet if you wish, with very small scraps of tights fabric.

7 Make the trousers by sewing the two trouser pieces with right sides of the fabric together. Sew the inside seam first, starting at the ankle hem on one leg and ending at the ankle hem on the other. Next, stitch from the waist to the ankle hem on both outside legs – still working with the right sides together. Gather the trousers at the waist and the ankles with a tiny running stitch, or alternatively attach a thin shirring elastic using a running stitch.

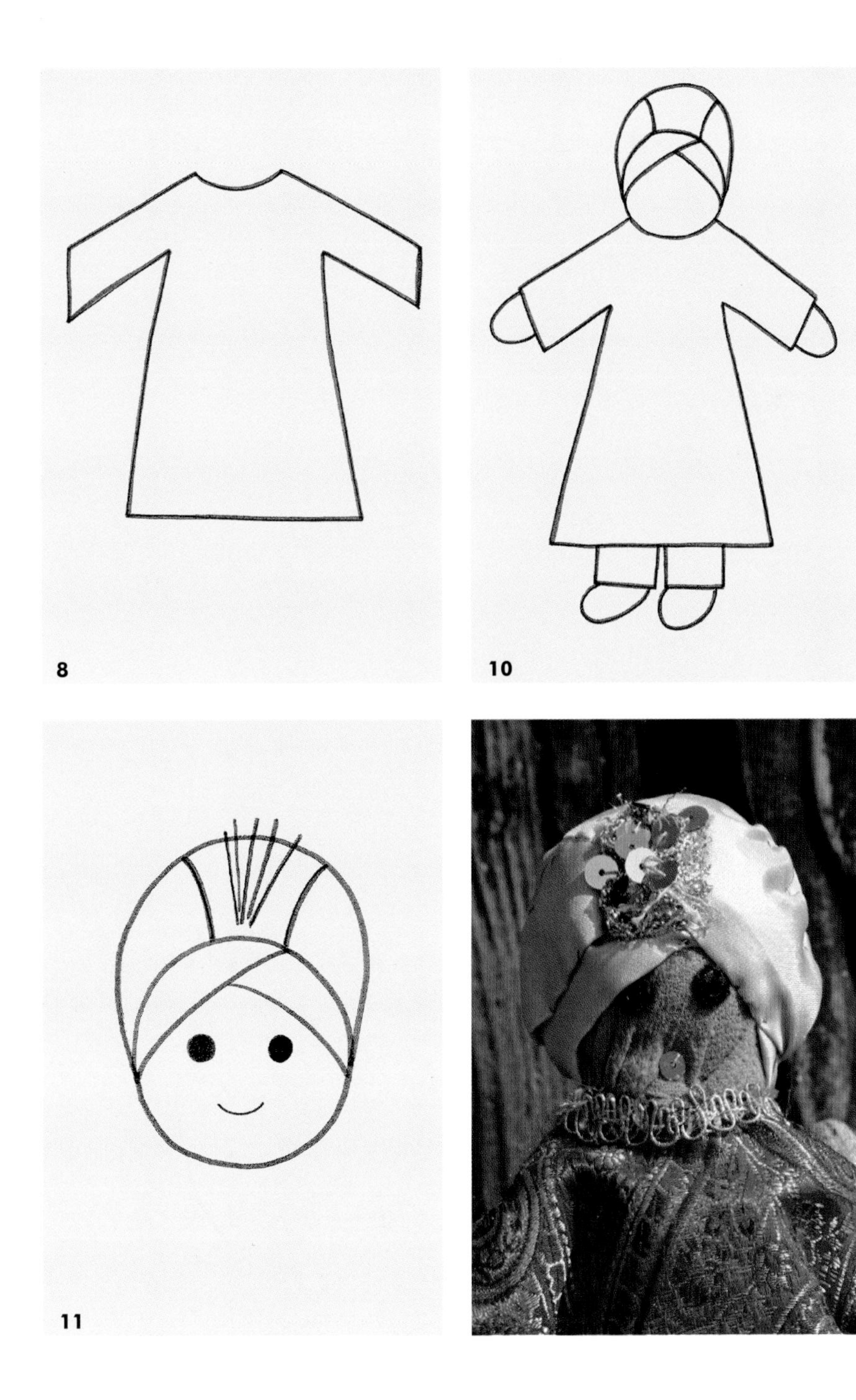

8 Make the tunic by sewing the two tunic pieces with right sides together. Start at the shoulder and stitch to the sleeve edge on both sides. Then stitch from the sleeve hem to the underarm, pivot, then stitch down to the hem at the lower edge of the tunic.

9 Add trim at the neck and the hem edge, and also down the central panel of the tunic if desired.

10 Fold a different-coloured fabric (to contrast with the tunic) around the doll's head to create a turban. Fold the fabric like an envelope and tuck the ends in at the front of the head. Fasten with stitches and embellish with sequins.

11 For the facial features, use sequins or stitch them in by hand. This example has one half of a press stud for the mouth.

Tights doll

This doll requires very little sewing and is simple and fun make, but you will need to be able to plait. The body is made from a pair of old tights – it doesn't matter if they are laddered – so this is a useful way to recycle! You will also need a small remnant of fabric for the dress.

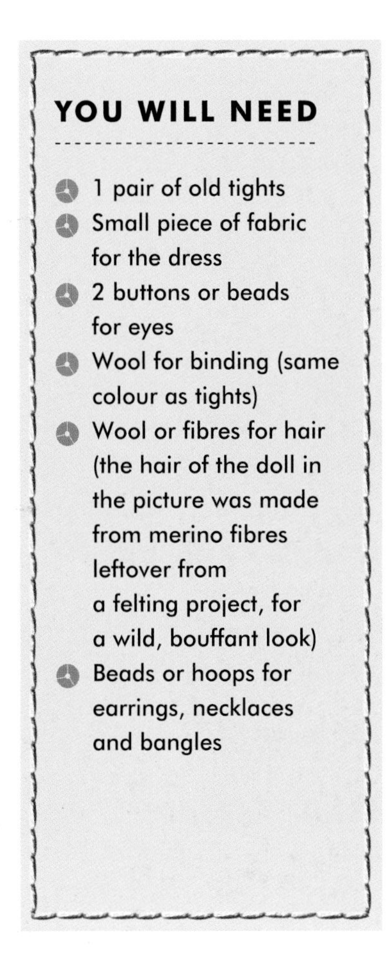

YOU WILL NEED

- 1 pair of old tights
- Small piece of fabric for the dress
- 2 buttons or beads for eyes
- Wool for binding (same colour as tights)
- Wool or fibres for hair (the hair of the doll in the picture was made from merino fibres leftover from a felting project, for a wild, bouffant look)
- Beads or hoops for earrings, necklaces and bangles

1 Cut a rectangular piece of fabric 20 x 36 cm (approx. 8 x 14in.) for the dress. Cut two smaller rectangles 16 x 5cm (approx. 6 x 2in.) for the straps of the dress.

2 Cut one of the legs of the pair of tights into three long strips. Knot the strips together at one end and plait them, tightly and evenly, taking care not to twist the plait. Finish with another knot when you reach the end. The knots at each end of the plait will become the feet.

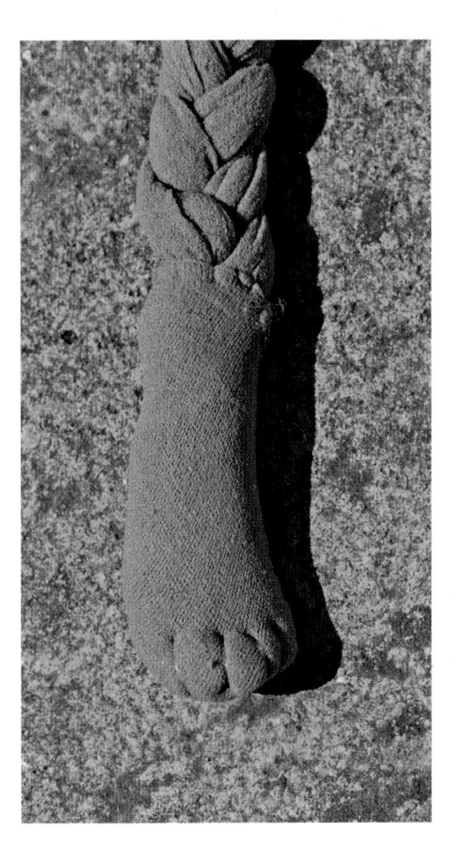

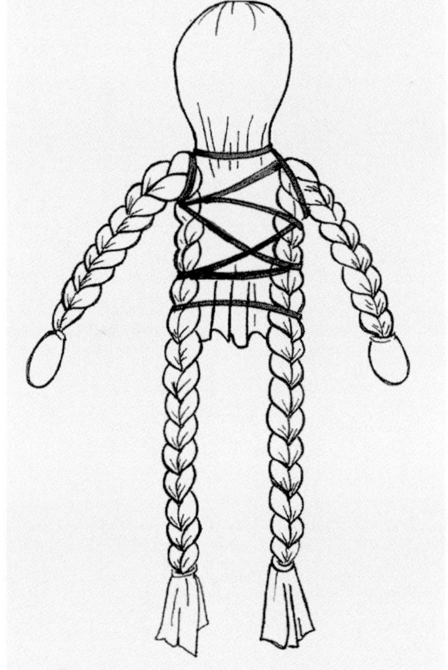

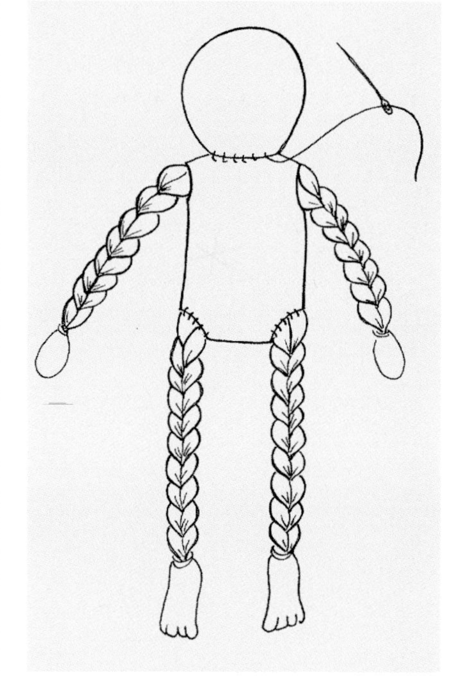

3 Fold the plait in half. Bind a small length of wool approximately 2.5cm (1in.) from the fold on each side, wrapping the wool around the plait several times then knotting it securely. This will form the wrists.

4 Cut the plait on the fold. You should now have two plaits, knotted at one end and bound at the other. Neatly fold in the cut ends, tucking them into the knots or the wool binding, to form little pads for feet and hands. Secure using a slip stitch. If you like, make long, straight stitches on the feet and pull them tight to form toes.

5 Taking the second leg of the pair of tights, cut out a circle as wide as the fabric will allow and prepare a handful of small scraps of the tights fabric. Create a 'ball' for the head by rolling the scraps into a wad and stretching the circle of fabric over it. Squeeze it into a head shape. Use tacking stitches to close up the fabric and ensure the stuffing doesn't fall out. Spread out the loose fabric below the head.

6 Position each plaited limb correctly in relation to the head, with the hand at one end and a foot at the other. Bind the middle section of the plaits to the loose material below the head with wool to form the base for the body.

7 Wrap the remains of the tights around the body to pad it out. When you have the size and shape you want secure the end of the fabric at the back with neat stitches. Stitch the neck to the newly-formed body. Stitch the limbs to the body to fix them in place.

8 Sew the merino fibres or wool strands to the head to give your doll a hairstyle, and attach beads or buttons for her eyes.

9 The dress shown here is not removable. Sew the two fabric pieces, with right sides together, to make the dress. Hem the lower edge and the armholes, and slip the dress onto the doll. Gently gather the neckline of the dress with neat row of running stitches.

10 Create two straps by stitching a seam along the length of the two smaller rectangles of fabric, with right sides together. Turn to the right side and press flat. Position the straps with the ends inside the dress and secure on the gathered top edge with one or two tiny stitches. If you want to you can fix the dress onto the body of the doll with tiny stitches along the gathered top edge of the dress.

Cone doll

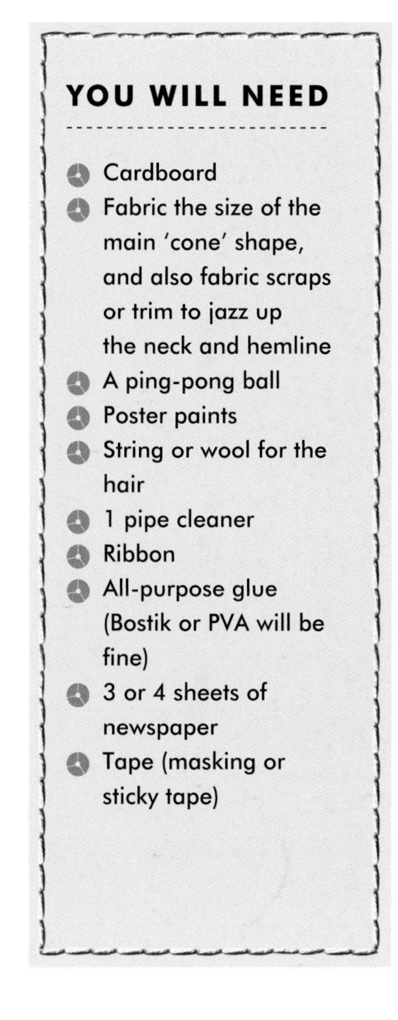
YOU WILL NEED

- Cardboard
- Fabric the size of the main 'cone' shape, and also fabric scraps or trim to jazz up the neck and hemline
- A ping-pong ball
- Poster paints
- String or wool for the hair
- 1 pipe cleaner
- Ribbon
- All-purpose glue (Bostik or PVA will be fine)
- 3 or 4 sheets of newspaper
- Tape (masking or sticky tape)

This doll is made from all recycled bits that you are very likely to have around the house. She is a good size – quite diddy – for sitting as an ornament on a tabletop or shelf, and could be used to deliver a message such as an invitation or a birthday greeting. The face is hand-painted, so each doll is unique. This doll doesn't require any sewing at all, so be prepared to get gluey fingers!

1 Make a paper pattern piece by drawing around a dinner plate. Cut the circle in half and form into a cone shape. Trim the bottom edge so that the cone stands up, then unroll. Use this pattern to cut a cone from both card and fabric.

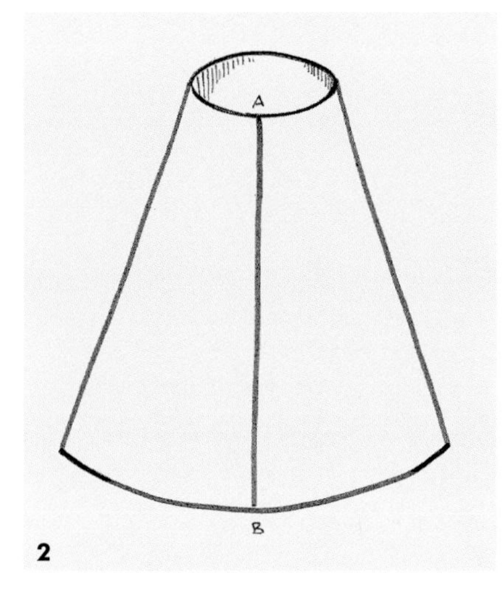

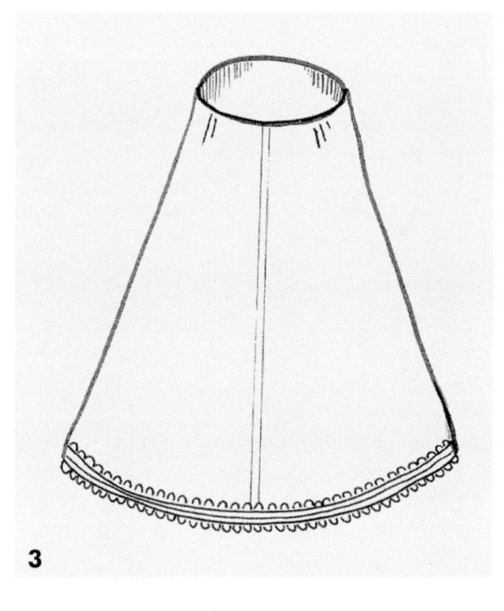

2 Join the cardboard piece at the back, making a line of glue from A to B, so that it creates a cone shape.

3 Cover the cone with fabric. Stick the fabric onto the card cone along the hem edge, the neck edge and the back 'seam' only. Stick trim along the neck and the hem for decoration.

4 Screw up the newspaper to make a ball which is the size of a clenched fist, and the right size to fit into the cone. Push the ball of paper to the top of the inside of the cone, and secure it to the walls of the cone with tape.

5 Use glue to stick the ping-pong ball to the top of the newspaper, through the 'neck' opening. Apply the face colour and leave the glue and the paint to dry.

6 Paint facial features on before gluing on string 'mound' for hair. On this one I just piled it onto the head until I liked the hairdo!

7 Wrap ribbon around a 16cm (6¼in.) length of pipe cleaner, to cover it.

8 Oversew the ends to join them together, and slip the newly created 'arms' over the head of the doll.

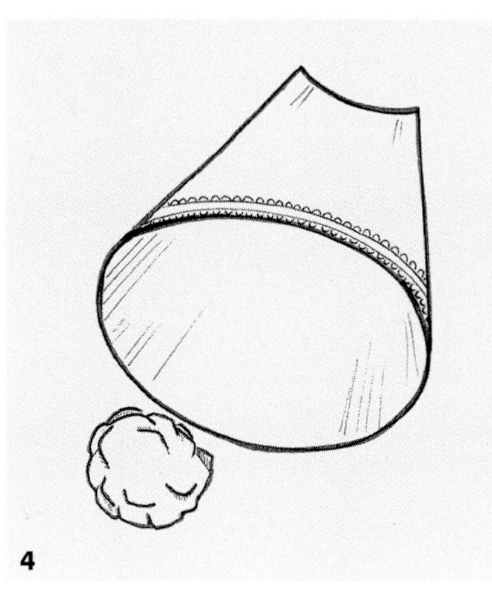
4

5

6

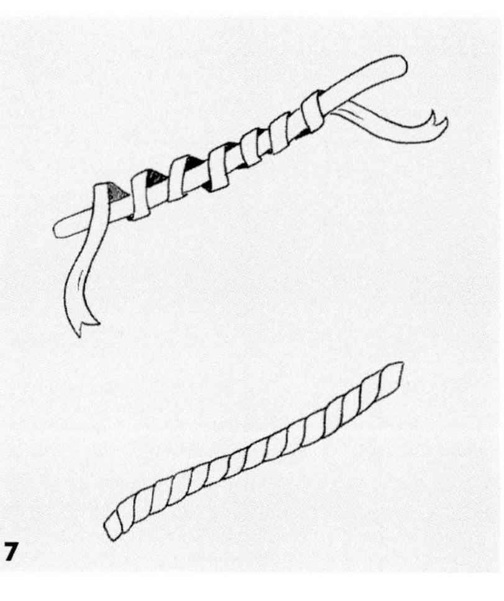
7

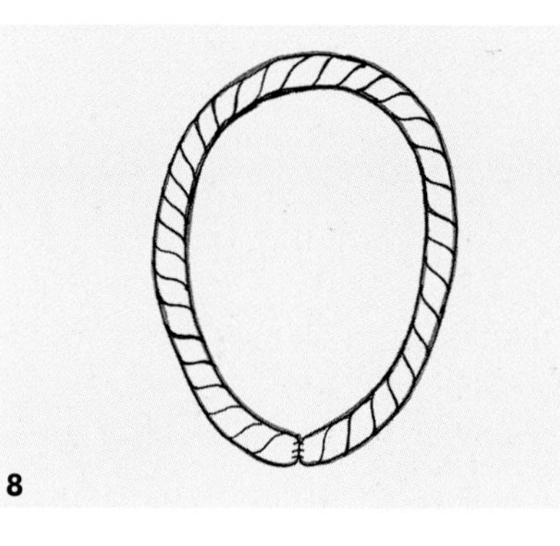
8

Peg doll

These are my favourite to make, probably because the outcomes are so adorable, and they are all unique. They are a good project for children too. My nan made bride dolls for us, and used a lock of her hair to make the dolls' hair. I use tiny prints for the dolls' dresses and I also like silk threads for hair as they are colourful and a nice soft texture. Use up any bits and bobs you have around.

YOU WILL NEED

- A wooden peg
- Fabric scraps – measurements for these are not given, being dependent on the size of peg
- Silks, wool or hair for hair
- Embellishments such as sequins and beads
- Felt-tip pens

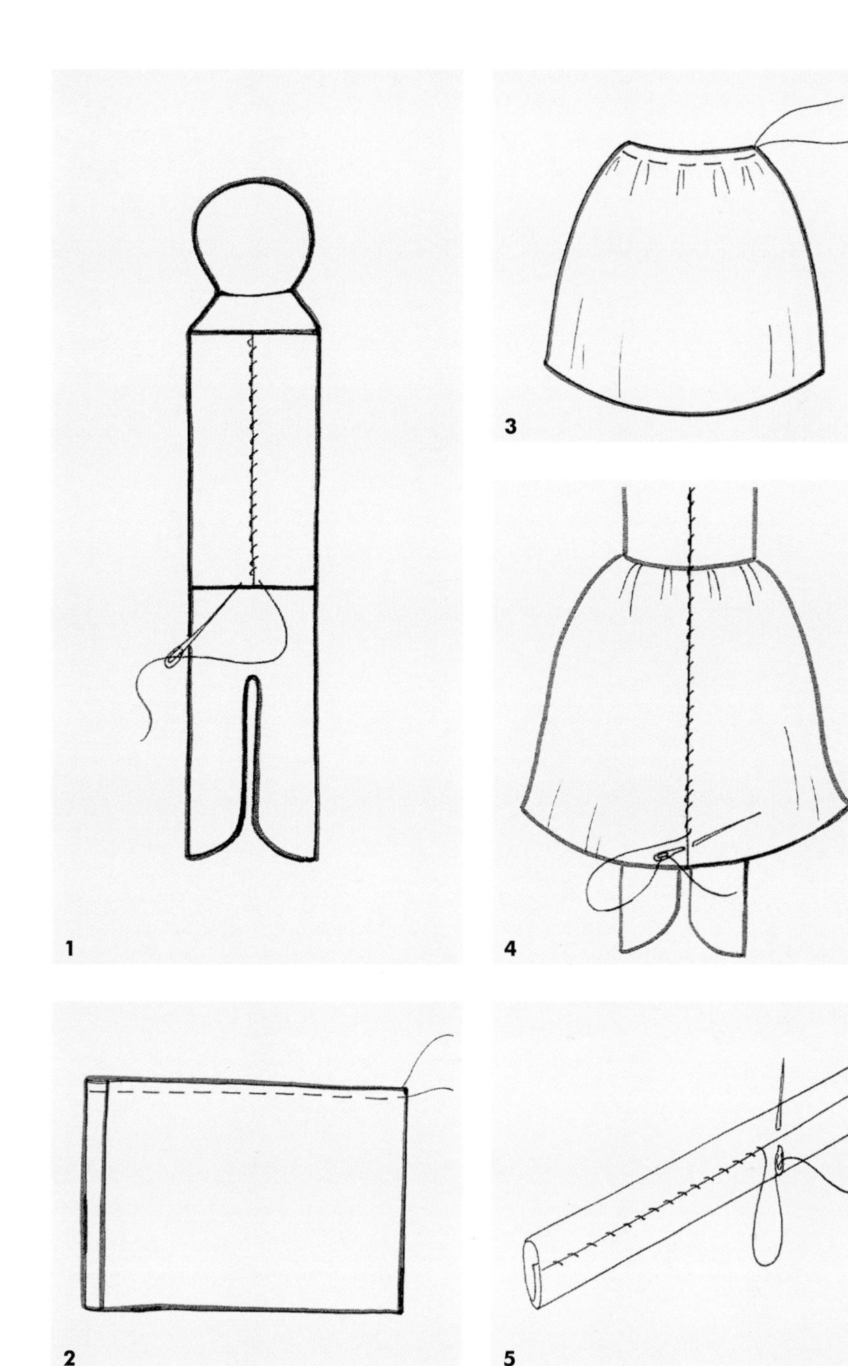

1 Use a square fabric piece to wrap around the body to form a top. Sew the back seam to keep in place as a tightly fitting garment.

2 Use a rectangular fabric piece twice the width of the square to create a skirt. Sew a running stitch along the top edge of the fabric.

3 Gather the fabric by gently easing it along the running stitch.

4 Place the newly formed skirt around the waist of the doll, and create a back seam by sewing with tiny stitches through two layers of fabric which should be overlapped by 0.5cm (¼in.).

5 Roll a rectangular piece three times as long as it is wide into a tube-shaped piece to create the arms of the doll.

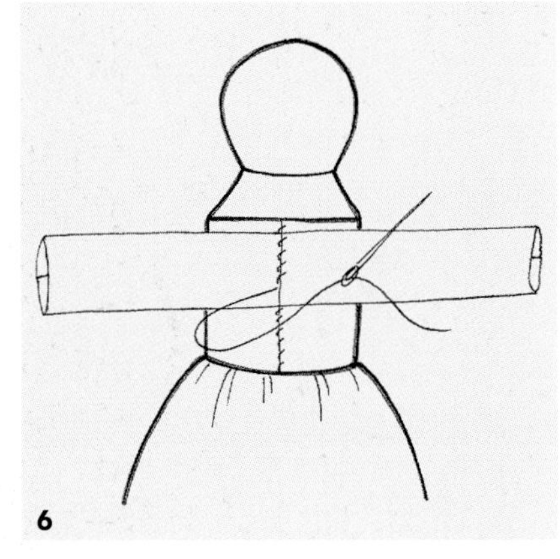

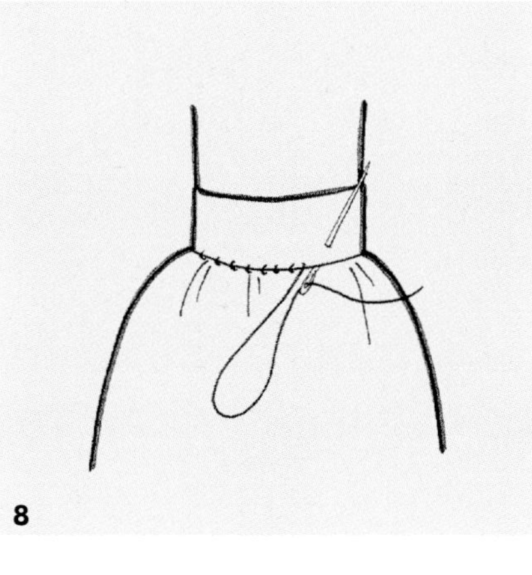

9

10

6 Attach the newly formed arms at the back of the doll, stitching through to the bodice fabric.

7 Fix the arms in your chosen position with more tiny stitches.

8 Use ribbon or trim to make a sash to cover the top edge of the skirt. Stitch the ribbon to the skirt with tiny stitches.

9 Glue on your chosen hairdo. Draw on a felt-tip face.

10 Two heart shapes look like slippers. Draw this with felt tip onto the type of peg that comes with a base, made especially for crafting.

From an original design by Jasmine, aged 8.

Part 2
Inspiration

6. Art dolls

Woodland creature by Sophia Simensky

Sophia Simensky is a visual artist and scenographer, working in the areas of performance and installation. She is interested in 'the fascination of the unusual and its exhibition'. Sophia makes theatre props and costumes and art, and created this 'rabbit girl' to be both charming and unsettling at the same time!

The doll is constructed from a rigid metal frame which is covered in papier mâché and then faux fur. The face is hand-painted and the eyes are small marbles.

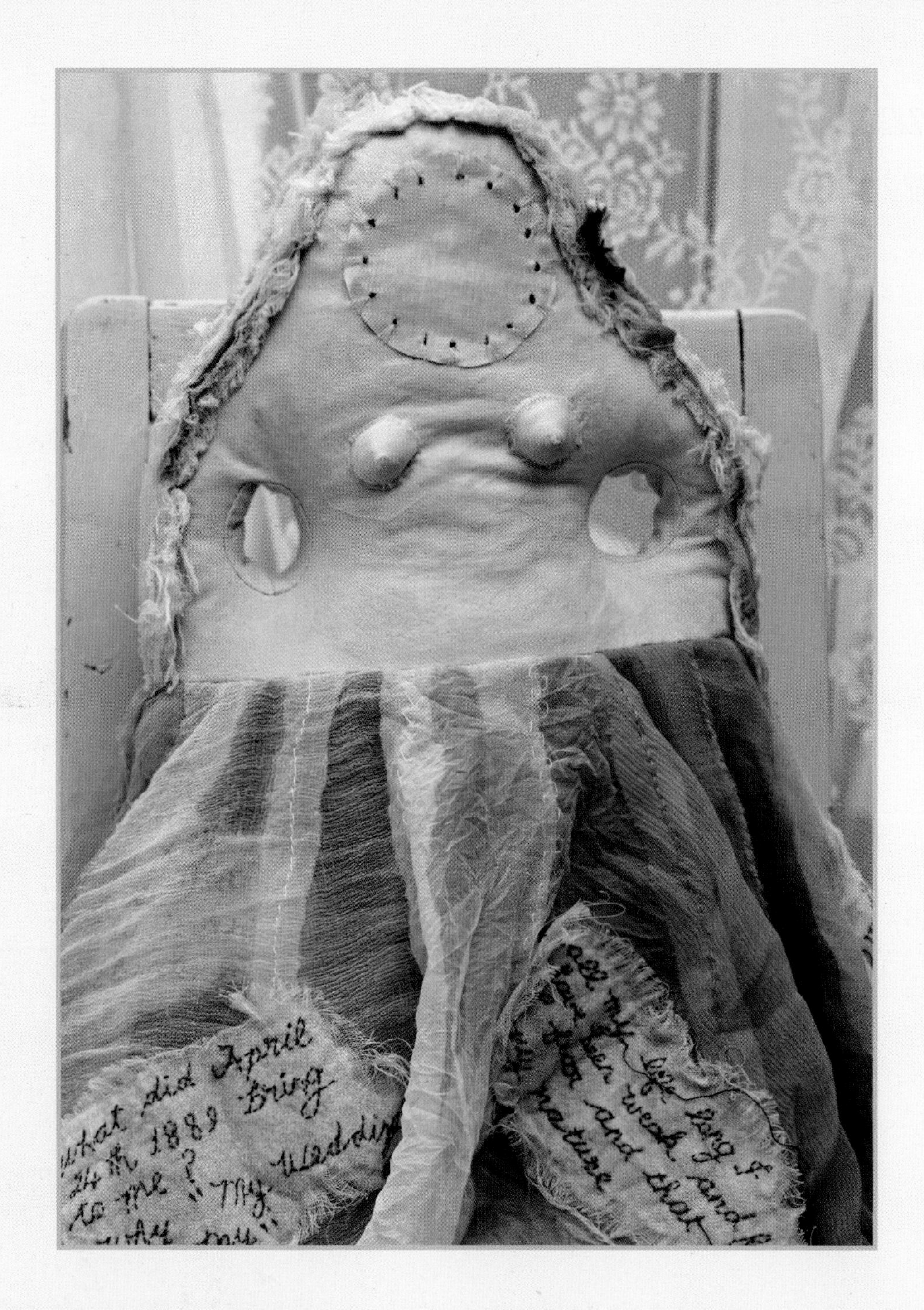
what did April
24th 1889 Bring
to me? "My Wedding
life long I
weak and
and that
nature

Memory skirt doll by Angela Smith

Angela Smith is an artist with a fashion background. She works mainly with fabric, and loves the history and intrigue that old objects bring; storytelling often features in her artwork. There is an interesting story behind her 'memory skirt doll'. Angela found a fascinating Victorian journal at a boot fair, written by a widow who was heartbroken by her loss. Angela was inspired to make this doll to represent the woman who wrote the diaries. She has made the doll's face featureless, representing the fact that the history of the writer of the diaries is partly speculation, and her skirt is many-layered, making reference to 'many-layered' Russian dolls as the woman was born in Russia. The skirts are stitched with words from the journal; quotes such as 'time heals the sorrow, but only intensifies the blank' are sewn with tiny red chain stitches.

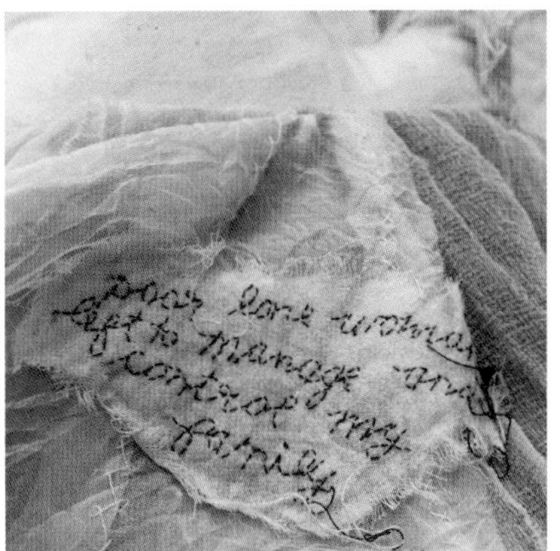

Positive and negative doll by Zoe Clifford

Zoe Clifford is an artist and dollmaker who specialises in soft sculpture and experimental dolls. She recently exhibited a 'Pearly Queen' doll in her local Hackney art show, and is interested in costume – our 'second skin', as she puts it – and how it enables us to perform a 'role'.

Her double-ended doll, which is around 60cm (23½in.) tall and hand-embroidered, is inspired by Greek mythology – representing Lady Luck and Nemesis, the enforcer of justice and goddess of retribution.

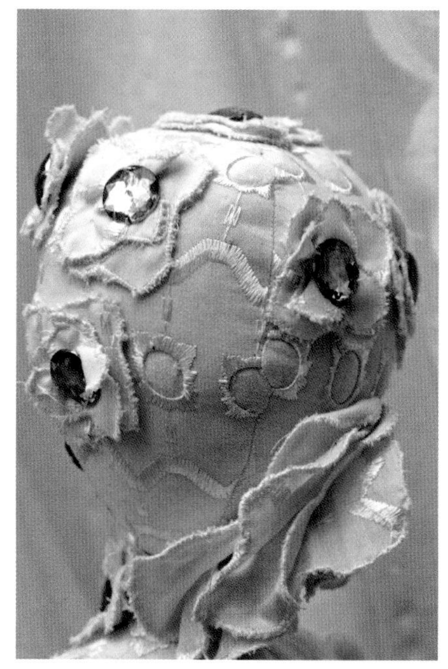

7. Doll makers

Abigail Brown

Abigail spent a large amount of time as a child in the company of her grandma, an incredibly talented, hardworking seamstress, in a house strewn with loose threads and scraps of fabric.
There is nothing more natural to Abigail than to work with fabric, using it to give life to the little creatures that form in her mind. Continuing to work in this way, she feels forever connected to her childhood and the wonderful days she spent with her grandma. She is a constant collector of fabrics, either bought new or used items she gathers and gives new life to. Her work centres around animals because they fascinate and inspire her.

Abigail studied a BA in Surface Decoration and Printed Textiles, graduating in 2003. After working as a designer and illustrator of children's books, childrenswear, stationery and greetings cards, she established herself as a textile artist. She has sold her work through many beautiful stores including Liberty of London, Takashimaya in New York, Bensimon in Paris, and through smaller but equally exquisite boutiques the world over.

---

abigail-brown.co.uk

Samantha Bryan

Samantha is a mixed-media artist based in West Yorkshire with a degree in Design, Crafts and Mixed Media. She has gained both national and international recognition and created work for display in large solo exhibitions, for public-art projects, and for both private and public collections.

She creates suspended, wall-mounted and freestanding sculptures of 'fairies' with machine-like contraptions. She tries to imagine the requirements that would be involved in 'fairy life' and is inspired by Victorian gadgetry and invention. Her sculptures evoke a sense of nostalgia, escapism and make-believe.

Each sculpture is laboriously created using a range of techniques including metalworking, woodworking and hand-stitching. The figures are built around a wire skeleton, and the bodies are made from pieces of leather stitched together. Knitted elements are sometimes also incorporated as part of the 'body-suit'. The heads are moulded out of air-drying paper clay. Samantha spends a lot of time sourcing items with which to embellish the figures, to produce items such as helmets, ear muffs, goggles and wings.

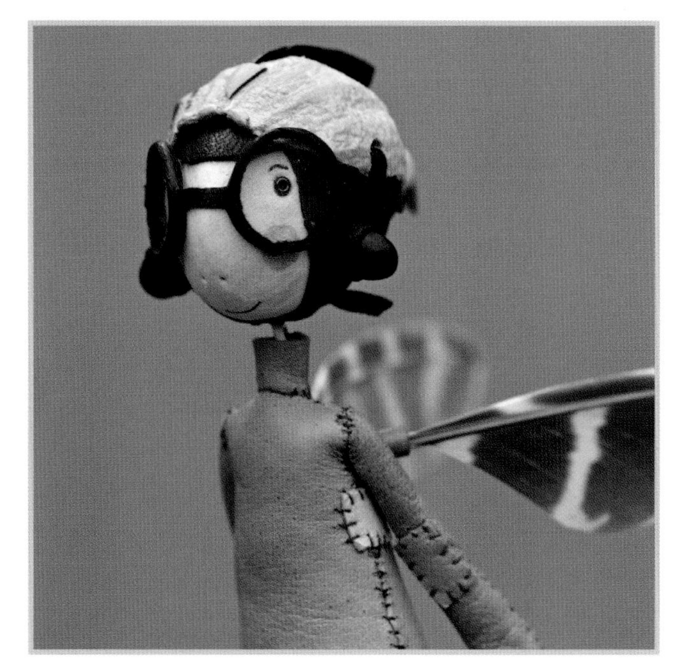

The machine-like contraptions are constructed using mainly brass tubing, wire and sheets. These materials are manipulated into shape and silver-soldered in place. The metal structures are then chemically treated to give the impression of age.

---

brainsfairies.co.uk

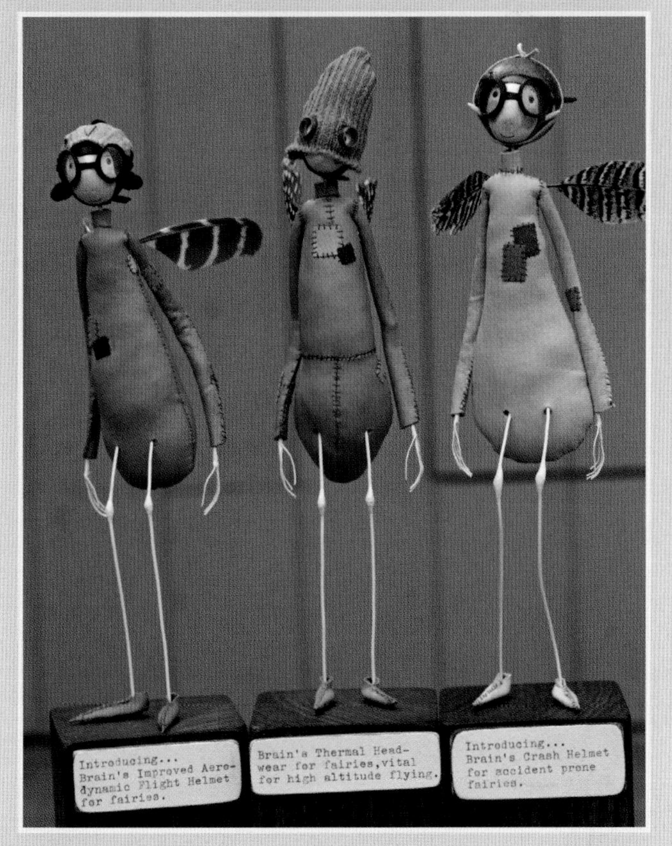
Introducing...
Brain's Improved Aero-
dynamic Flight Helmet
for fairies.
Brain's Thermal Head-
wear for fairies,vital
for high altitude flying.
Introducing...
Brain's Crash Helmet
for accident prone
fairies.

Rita Pinheiro

Matilde Beldroega is a brand of dolls and soft toys created, designed and handmade by Rita Pinheiro. After completing her degree in fine arts, Rita decided to make her passion (and hobby) for designing and making fabric dolls into her profession. Her company name comes from her cat Matilde, and the edible plant beldroega (purslane in English) used in a popular soup in Alentejo, Portugal, where she lives.

Matilde Beldroega's toys are designed for children of all ages, including adults as well, to be companions, to endure in time. 'As a child I played a lot with rag dolls, and my favourite ones were made by my paternal grandmother, who was a real source of inspiration. Making dolls is a good excuse for me to continue to play with dolls as an adult.' She uses natural materials: 100% cotton fabrics, linen, fabric wools and velvet wools, among others.

Each of Rita's creations is designed and produced as one-of-a-kind. 'I never make two toys alike or repeat the same solutions over and over. I love to accept customer orders and special requests. It's always a challenge and a pleasant way to see my work through other people's eyes.'

Matildebeldroegablog.com

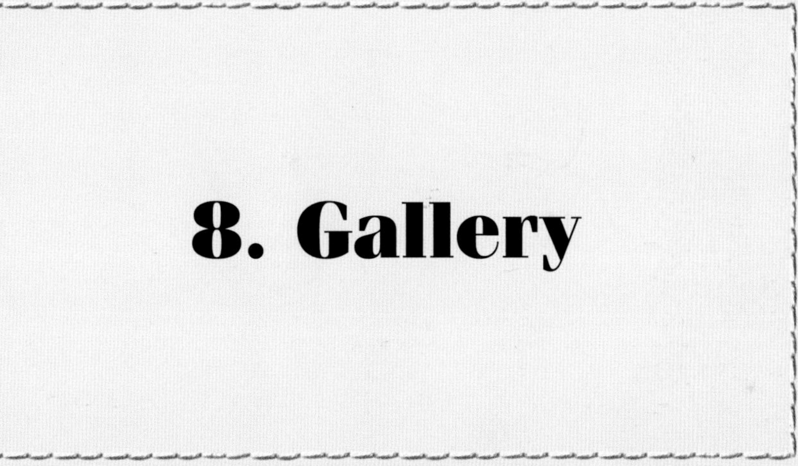

8. Gallery

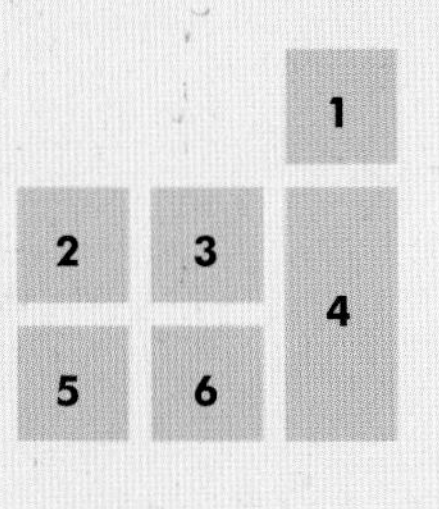

Doll on p.124 by Emily Durham

1 *Doll,* Laura Hoile

2 *Girly girl teddies,* Irene Strange

3 *Mirandês donkey and orange cat,* Ana Rita Pinhero Carolino Marques dos Reis

4 *Patch doll,* Irene Strange, www.irenestrange.co.uk. Inspired by Tim Burton's Sally Stitches.

5 *Little pink-pig*, Ana Rita Pinhero Carolino Marques dos Reis, www.matildebeldrogablog.com

6 Detail from doll by Holly Adams

1 *Fox*, Abigail Brown, www.abigail-brown.co.uk

2 *Cherry Sparkle*, Cherry Hurren

3 *Lola Stripes and Naomi Safetypins*, Cherry Hurren, www.cherryhurren.co.uk

1 *Peg dolls,* Jasmine and Lucas Stewart

2 *Doll,* Sarah Chin

3 *Neela*, Lesley Cameron

4 *Tisha*, Lesley Cameron,

www.lesleyjanedolls.etsy.com

1 *Lollilady and Miss Kate*, Jen Musatto, www.themdollz.com. Photo: Pamela Lopez, www.PLportraiture.com

2 *Doll*, Emily Durham

3 *Doll*, unknown maker

GET CREATIVE!

Flat dolls, peg dolls, rag dolls – use your imagination and get started!

Illustrations by Emelie Svensson.

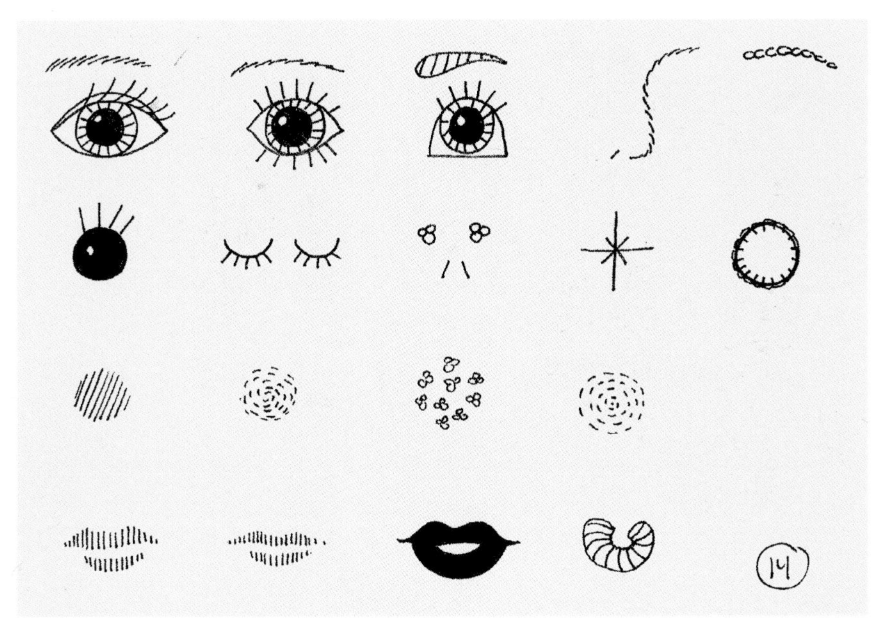

FACIAL FEATURES

To make a face for your creature, try stitching (in embroidery silks, sewing thread or wool), appliqué, or using buttons for eyes, cheeks and mouths.

You might like to use the examples shown here as a guide. Always put the face on after the head has been stuffed (with the exception of the Painted fabric dolls on p.23. Practise first, using a scrap of the same fabric, and to help position stitching, make a mark using a soft pencil first.

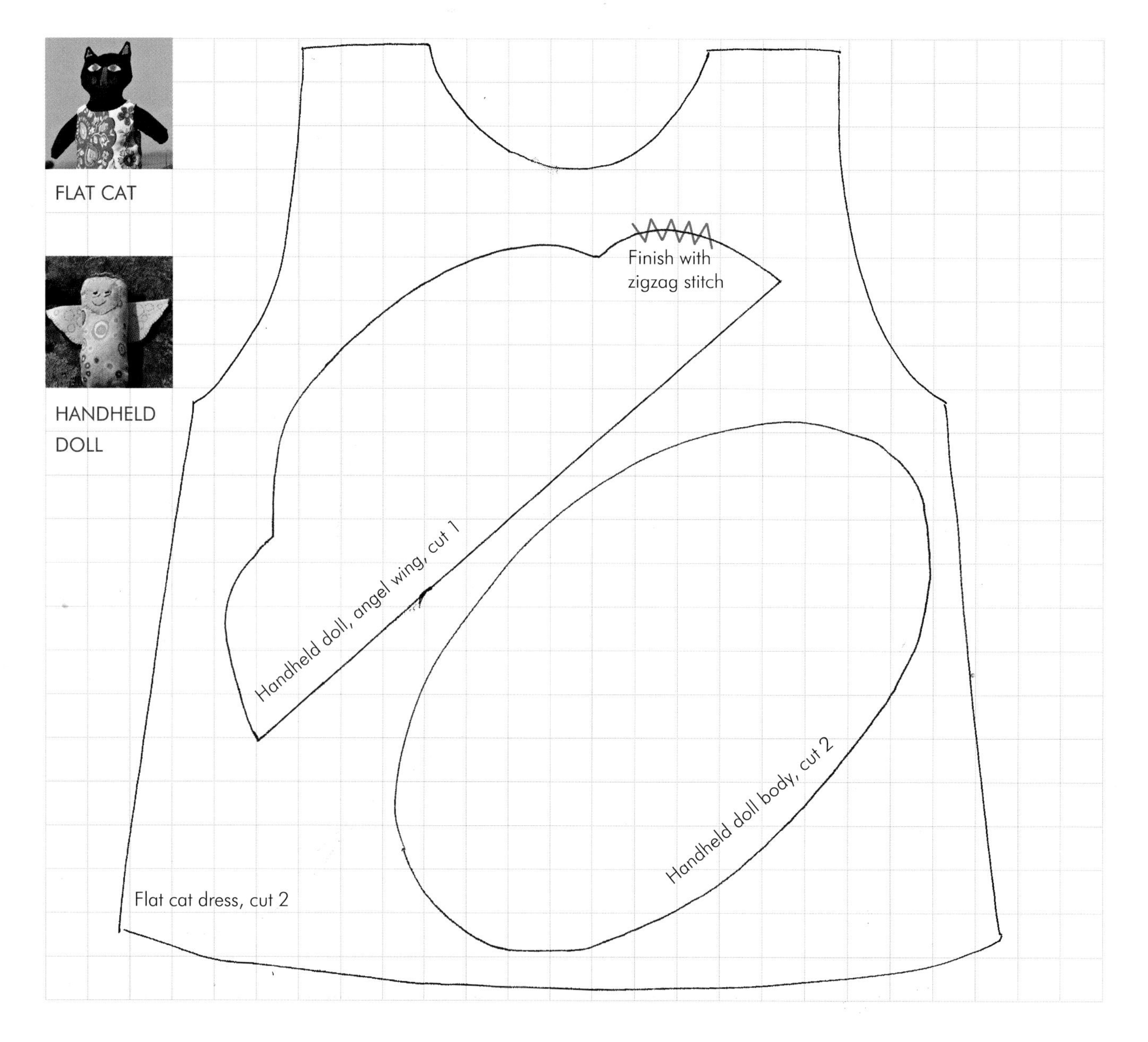
FLAT CAT
HANDHELD DOLL
Finish with zigzag stitch
Handheld doll, angel wing, cut 1
Handheld doll body, cut 2
Flat cat dress, cut 2

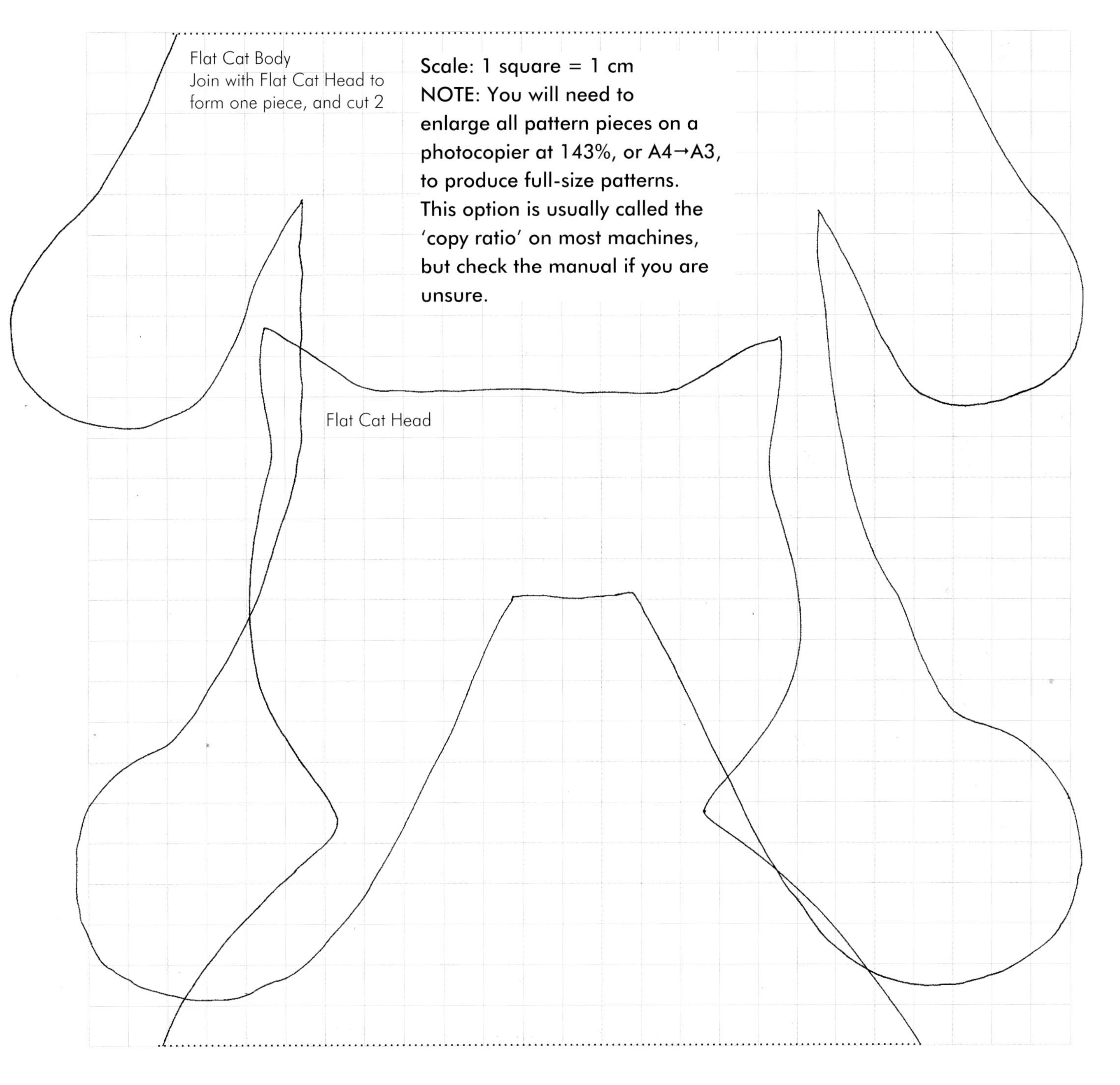
Flat Cat Body
Join with Flat Cat Head to
form one piece, and cut 2
Scale: 1 square = 1 cm
NOTE: You will need to
enlarge all pattern pieces on a
photocopier at 143%, or A4→A3,
to produce full-size patterns.
This option is usually called the
'copy ratio' on most machines,
but check the manual if you are
unsure.
Flat Cat Head

MAN AND LADY DOLLS

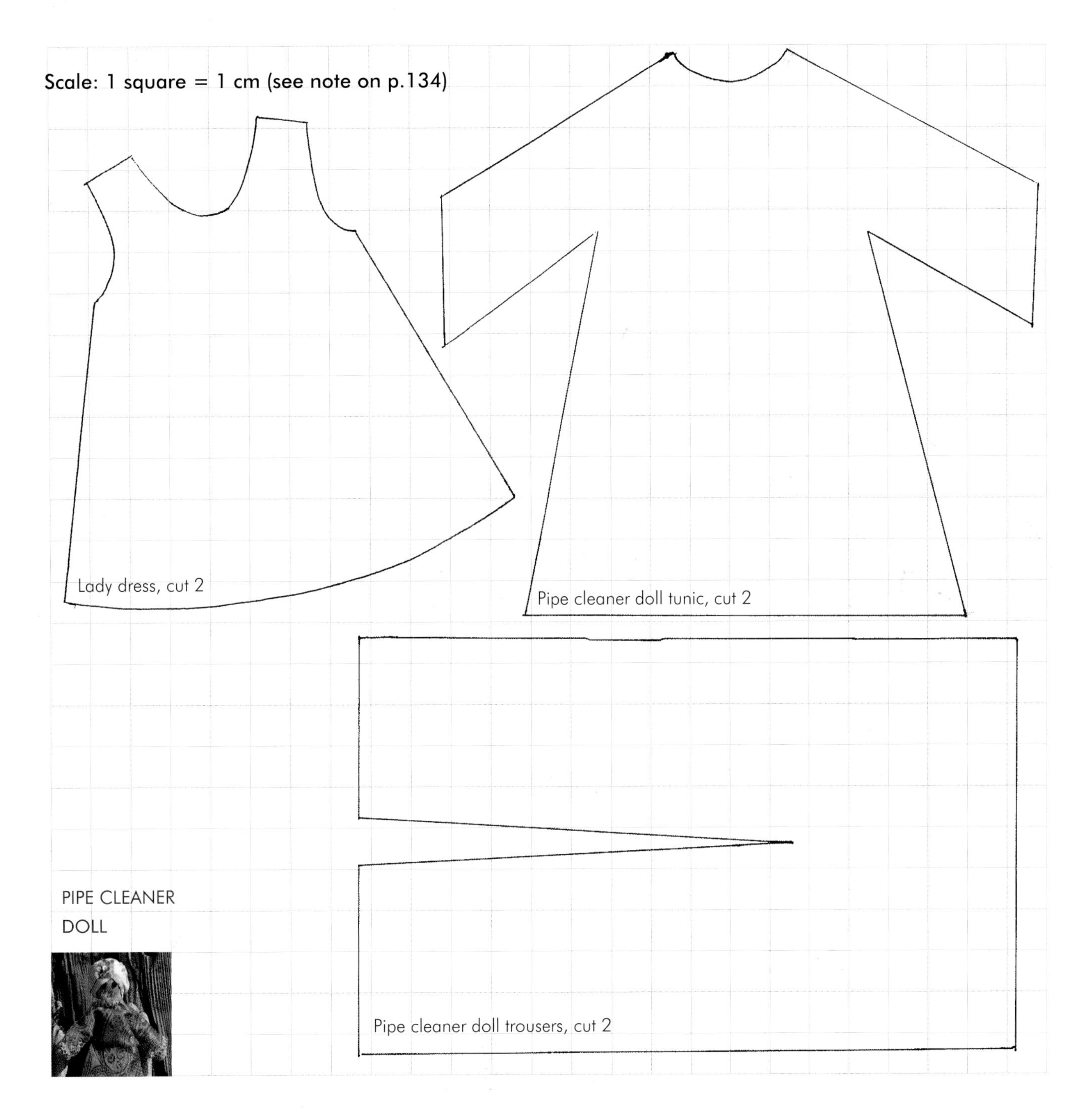
Scale: 1 square = 1 cm (see note on p.134)
Lady dress, cut 2
Pipe cleaner doll tunic, cut 2
Pipe cleaner doll trousers, cut 2
PIPE CLEANER
DOLL

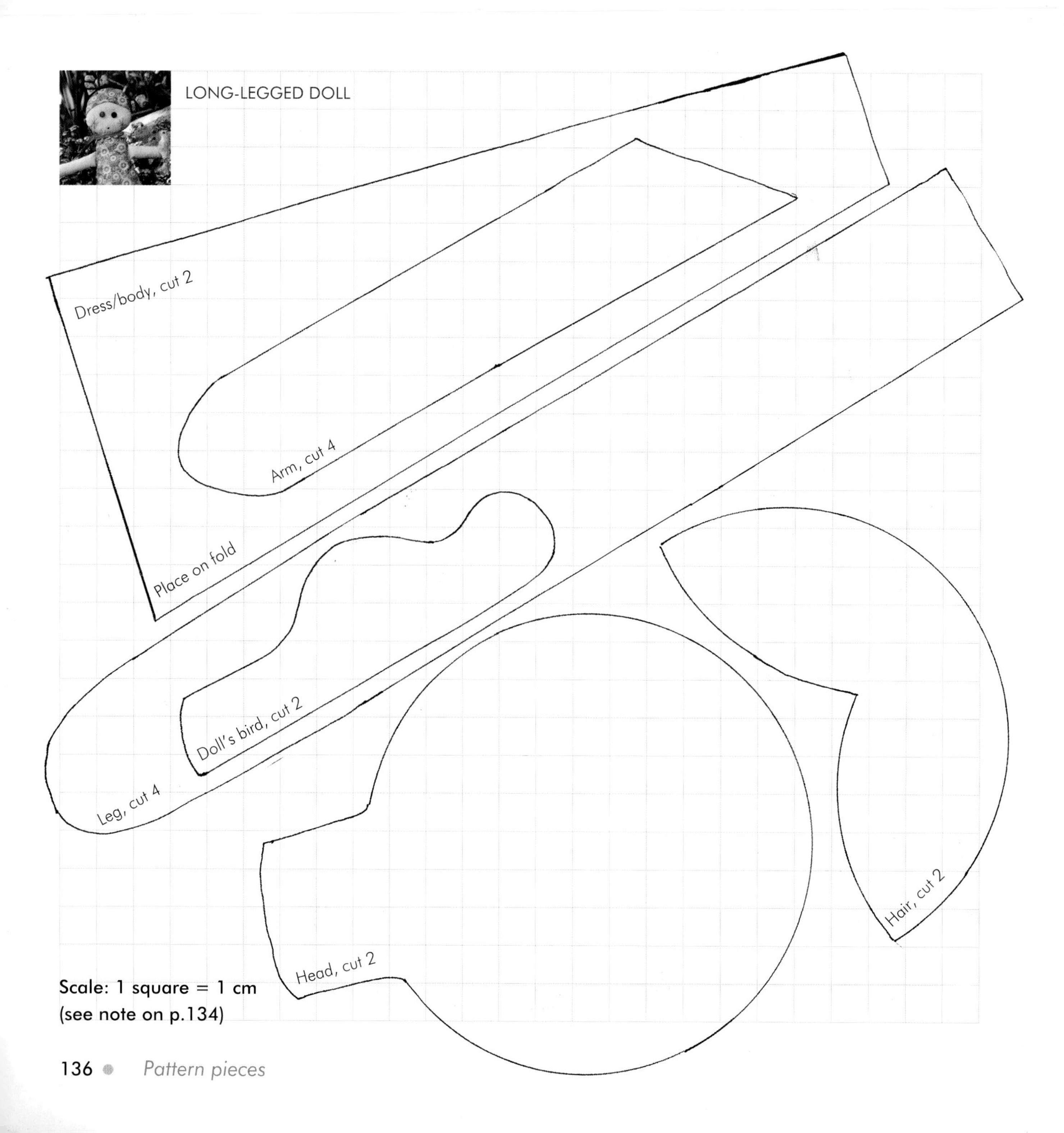
LONG-LEGGED DOLL
Dress/body, cut 2
Place on fold
Arm, cut 4
Leg, cut 4
Doll's bird, cut 2
Head, cut 2
Hair, cut 2
Scale: 1 square = 1 cm
(see note on p.134)

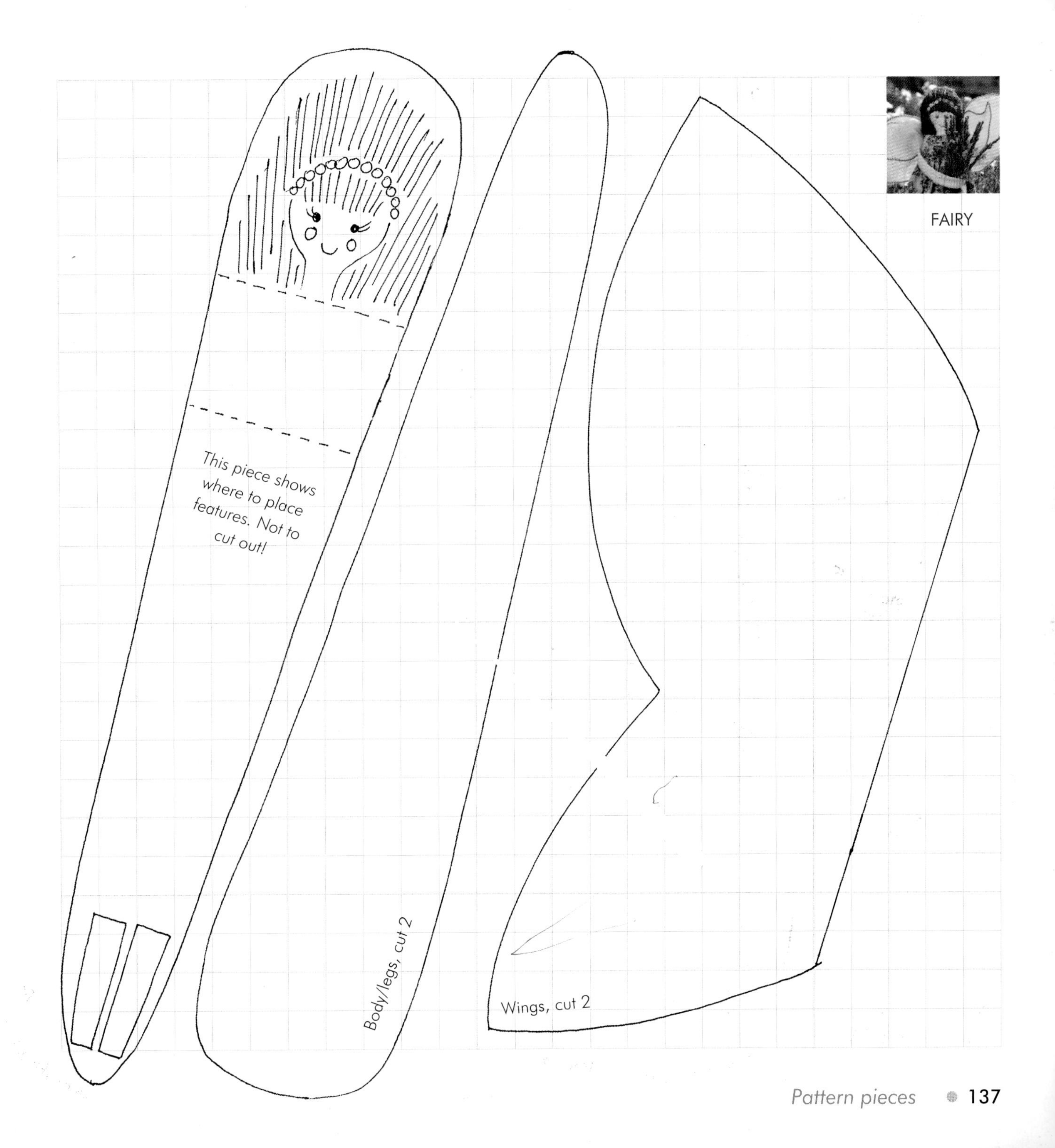
FAIRY
This piece shows where to place features. Not to cut out!
Body/legs, cut 2
Wings, cut 2

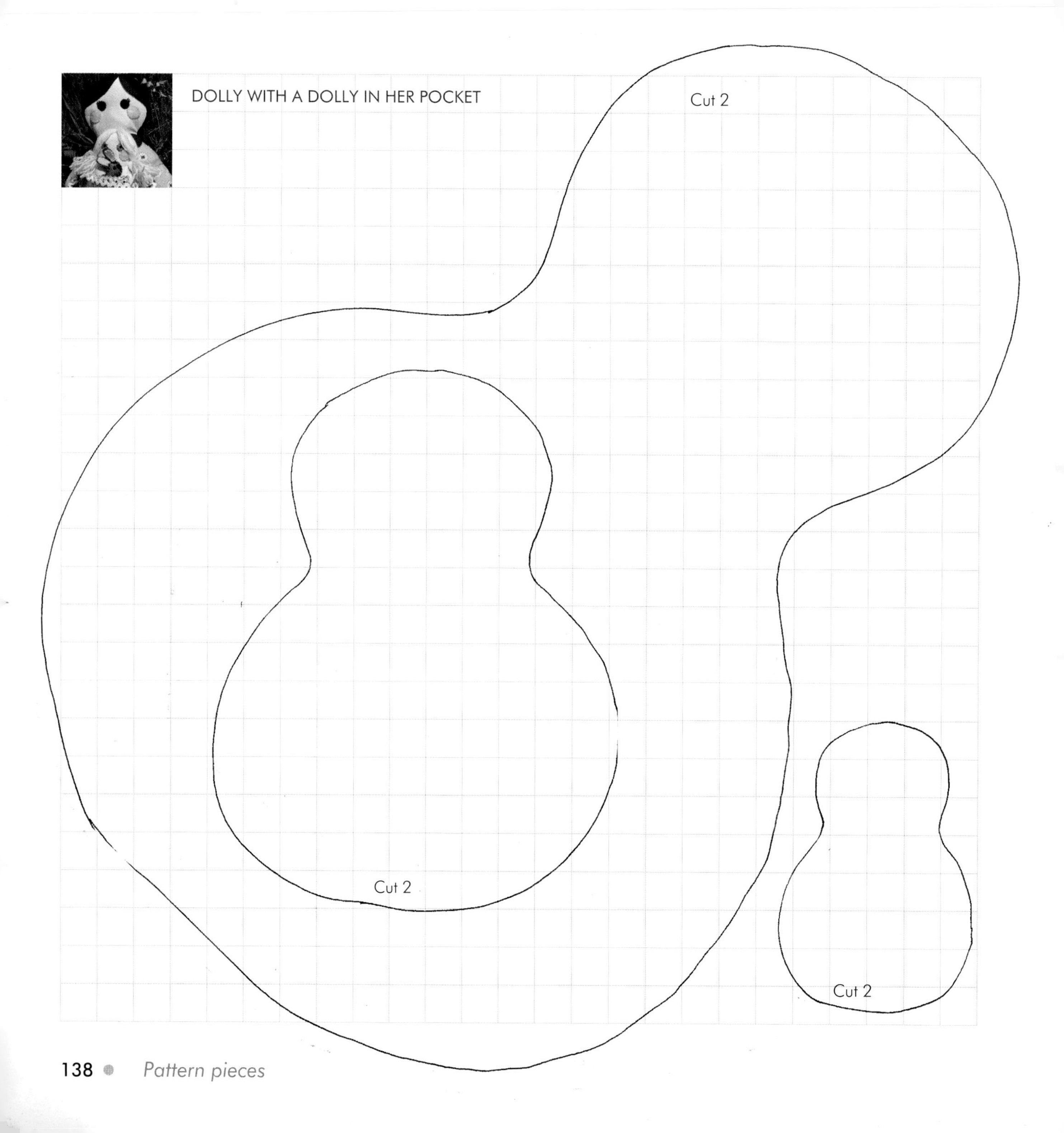
DOLLY WITH A DOLLY IN HER POCKET
Cut 2
Cut 2
Cut 2

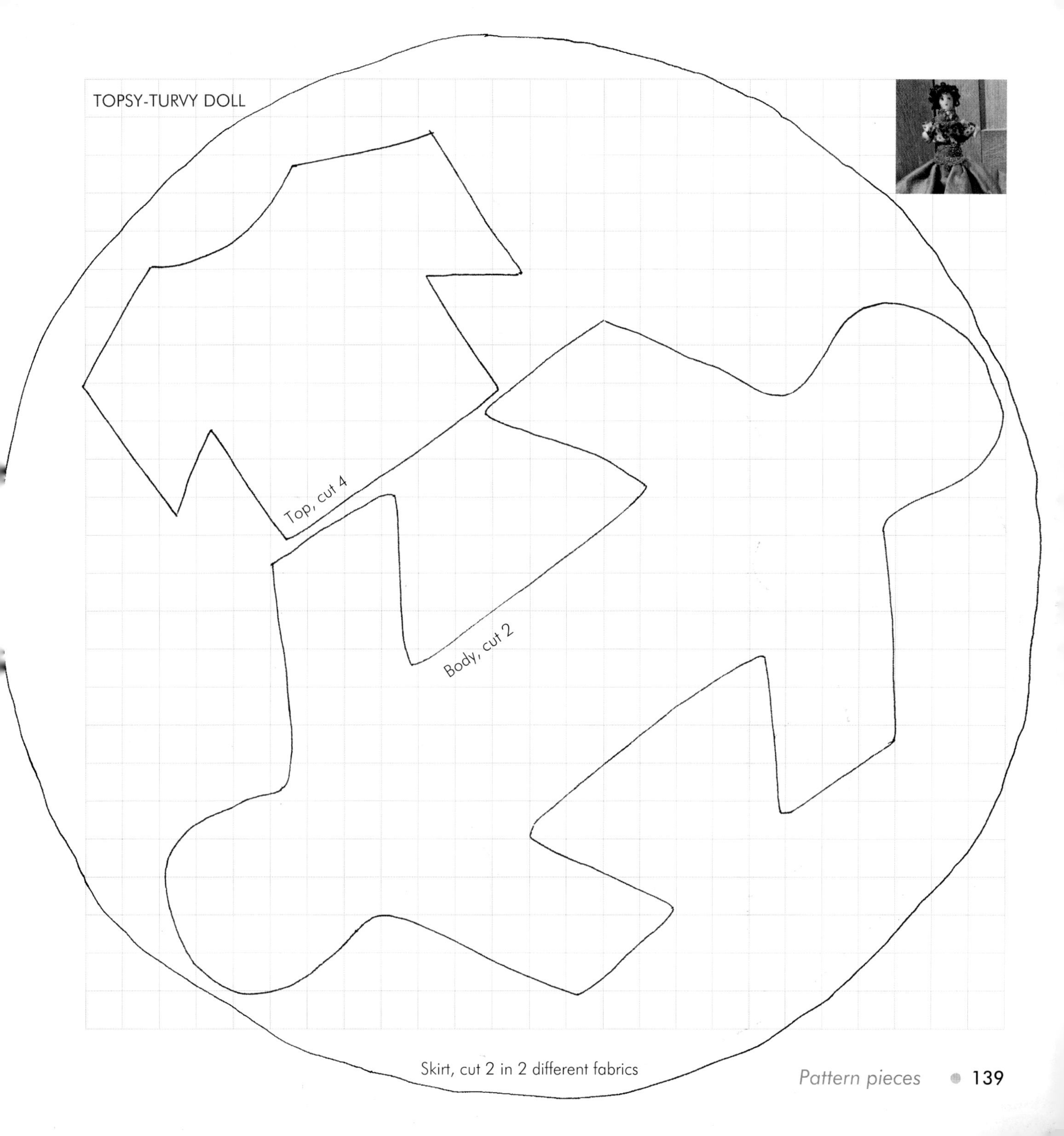
TOPSY-TURVY DOLL
Top, cut 4
Body, cut 2
Skirt, cut 2 in 2 different fabrics

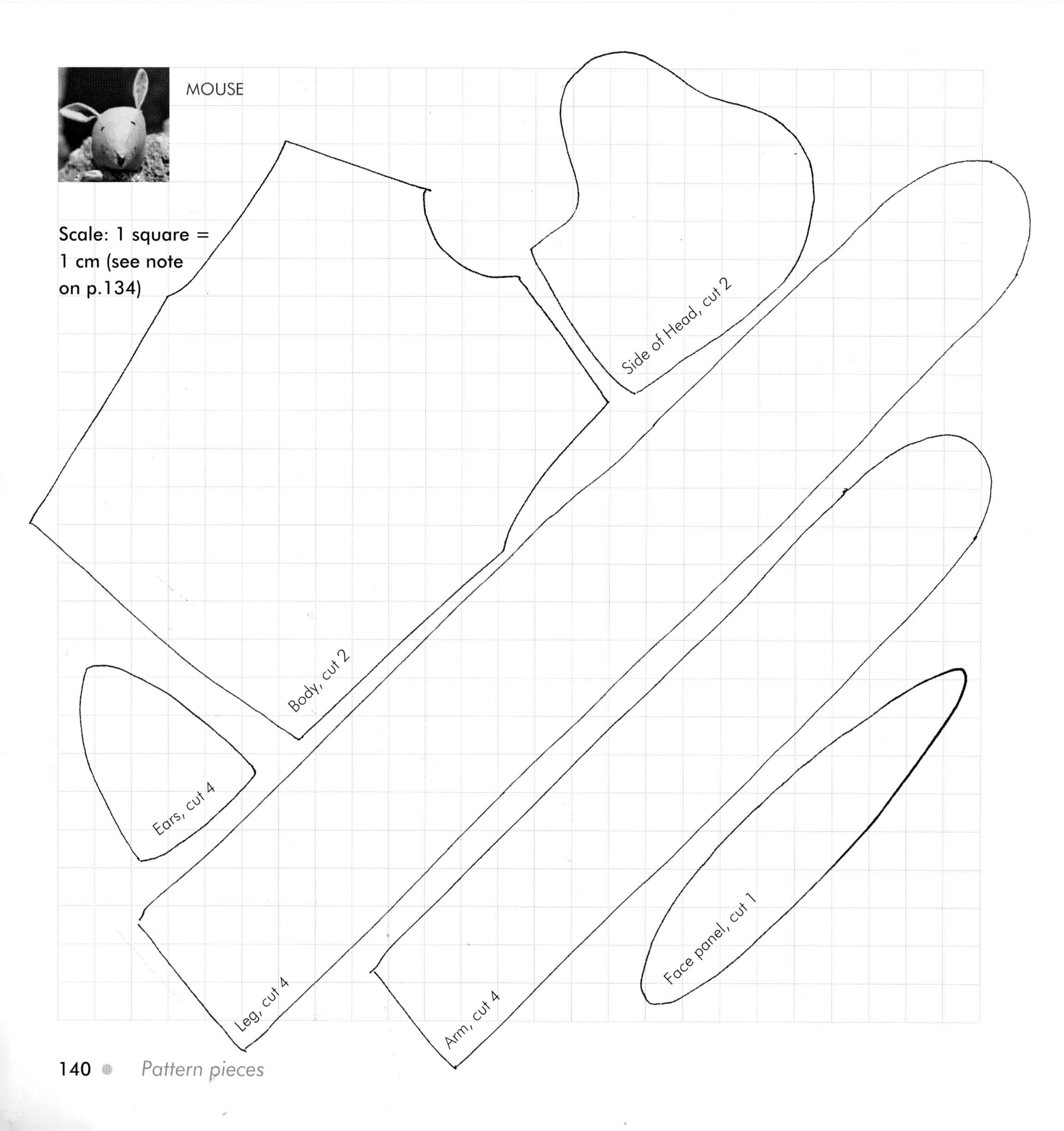
MOUSE
Scale: 1 square = 1 cm (see note on p.134)
Side of Head, cut 2
Body, cut 2
Ears, cut 4
Leg, cut 4
Arm, cut 4
Face panel, cut 1

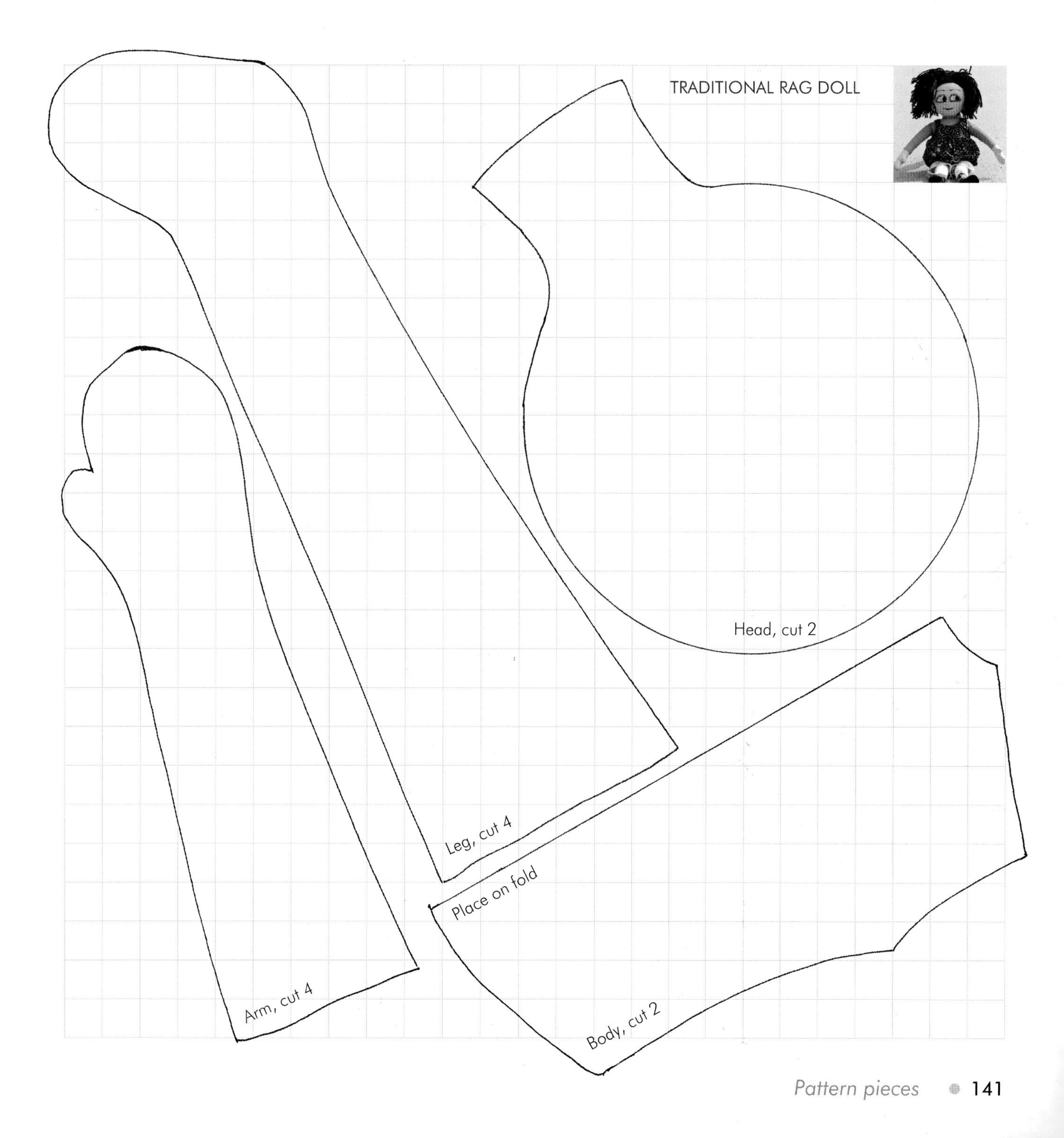
TRADITIONAL RAG DOLL
Head, cut 2
Leg, cut 4
Arm, cut 4
Place on fold
Body, cut 2

Glossary

appliqué The ornamental application of one fabric to another to create pattern or decoration.

casing A channel formed by folding an extended edge or any extra strip to house elastic or a drawstring.

embroidery silks Threads that are thicker and more glossy than sewing threads; used for decortive work.

embellishments Any decoration used on the surface of a fabric – beads, sequins, buttons, braid etc.

flat doll A doll that is generally made from two pattern pieces that are identical in shape. The doll has no shaping and is therefore flat.

gather Sewing a straight stitch through one layer of fabric and then bunching the fabric 'along' the resulting thread, to create gathers in the fabric.

hem A finish at an edge of fabric made by folding the raw edge under and stitching it down.

lining A concealed layer of fabric that lines the outer layer, often to preserve shape and give a neat finish at edges such as necklines.

merino fibres Sometimes called merino or woollen 'tops', these are woollen fibres used to spin into yarn or make felt. They are used to make hair in this book (see, for example, p.96).

oversew A straight stitch often used to close a gap and to join two pieces of fabric together.

pattern piece Paper templates, such as those provided in this book, that can be traced off and enlarged as a guide for cutting the fabric pattern pieces required.

pompoms A woollen trim of bauble shapes – woollen pompoms can also be handmade.

remnants Fabric off-cuts or scraps of fabric.

soft sculpture Any 3D piece made from fabric – usually stuffed to give it its shape.

stuff To fill (a doll) with shop-bought stuffing, wadding, rags or old tights in order to create a firm shape to the doll.

stump doll A doll made from a simple 'stump' shape that has no limbs – although these are sometimes added on as separate pieces.

right sides The instruction 'right sides together' means that the good side/best side of one fabric piece is placed touching the good side of the other fabric piece when sewing one piece to the other. This ensures the right side of the fabric is on show and the stitches are hidden on the inside.

rag doll A doll made from fabric. It need not be made of rags, but traditionally could be stuffed with rags.

tack A long, loose temporary hand stitch used to sew two layers together or to mark where permanent stitches should be placed.

Suppliers

Although you will hopefully be able to recycle and reuse fabric scraps and wools for the projects in this book, there will be times when you need to replenish supplies, so here are a few places to try.

www.knitrowan.com, for Rowan yarns.

www.littlecraftybugs.co.uk, for wooden pegs to make peg dolls as well as pipe cleaners and other bits.

www.vvrouleaux.com, for an enormous selection of trim, braid, ribbon and other embellishments.

www.cafeknit.co.uk, for yarn and wool including Debbie Bliss.

www.beyondfabrics.com, for a wide selection of retro prints.

www.hobbycraft.co.uk, for pipe cleaners, pegs for making dolls' eyes wadding and stuffing.

www.winifredcottage.co.uk, for best quality embroidery silks in every colour. The very friendly lady is available for phone orders on 01252 617667.

www.rosesrue.co.uk, for a large selection of wool, trims and lovely printed fabrics.

www.adelaidewalker.co.uk, for wool and silk fibres used for felt making but also great for dolls' hair.

www.textere.co.uk, for wool yarns, threads and embroidery silks.

1 *Monkeys with handstitched clothes made by Little Nanny Turner around 1969.*

2 *Bunny from project on pp.45–7.*

Index